Work

THIS IS IS!

Ian Ithurralde • Anne Ramkaran

Hodder & Stoughton

A MEMBER OF THE HODDER HEADLINE GROUP

British Library Cataloguing in Publication Data

Ithurralde, Ian
  This is IS!
  I. Title II. Ramkaran, Anne
  004. 0712041

ISBN 0 340 61103 0

First published 1996
Impression number   10 9 8 7 6 5 4 3 2
Year   1999   1998   1997   1996

Printed in Great Britain for Hodder & Stoughton Educational, a division of Hodder Headline Plc, 338 Euston Road, London NW1 3BH by Redwood Books, Trowbridge, Wilts.

Contents

Introduction

This book provides coverage of the theoretical aspects of GCSE courses in Information Systems and Information Technology. It will also be useful for those studying GNVQ courses. The book starts by examining the tools and techniques used in developing solutions to problems. In this section you will learn about the hardware and software which can be used when developing an IT solution. We have usually concentrated on what the hardware and software can do, rather than providing details of how it works. It is a good idea to read this section first so that you know what is available.

Here you can find out about different kinds of input and output devices and the various kinds of storage devices that are available. You will also find out about software including the operating system, computer languages and applications packages.

The book also covers data and how it can be stored. We have included an introduction to relational databases because many modern database packages can only be used effectively with some knowledge of database theory.

The section on information systems and the law covers current legislation relating to the use and misuse of data and software.

We look at developing information systems and provide examples of some of the methods used in analysis and design. We have selected case studies to provide a range of examples from those likely to be quite familiar, to those which will be outside the direct experience of most readers.

Within each chapter there are questions to test understanding of the subject content. Examination questions are grouped together at the back of the book and will provide a useful resource during the course and for revision purposes.

A glossary of terms used in the book is provided and this contains definitions of all the terms which appear in **bold** type.

Computers and Computer Systems

What makes a computer system?

A simple computer system consists of the computer itself, and other hardware devices which are attached to the computer. We usually call these extra devices **peripherals**. The photograph (below) shows a typical micro-computer system.

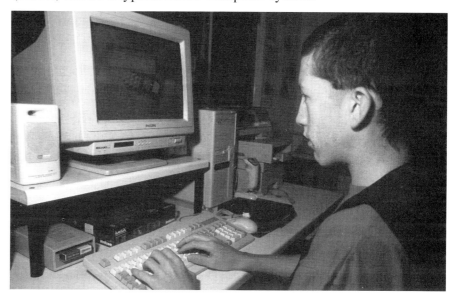

A micro-computer system.

The block diagram (Figure 1.1) shows the layout of the same micro-computer system.

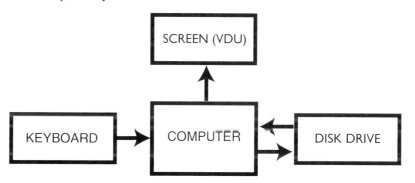

Figure 1.1 Hardware block diagram.

In this system the computer is attached to a screen, so that output can be displayed. It is attached to a keyboard so the user can type in instructions and data. It is also attached to a disk drive which is used to store programs and data on magnetic disk.

Notice the direction of the arrows on the diagram. These arrows show the direction of data movement. Data moves out of the computer to the screen so we call the screen an **output device**. Data moves from the keyboard into the computer so we call the keyboard an **input device**. The disk drive in the diagram is connected by two arrows, one in each direction. Data can move from the computer to the disk drive and also from the disk drive to the computer. The disk drive is a **storage device**. This type of diagram can be used to show any combination of hardware devices. In Figure 1.2 a printer, a mouse and another disk drive have been added.

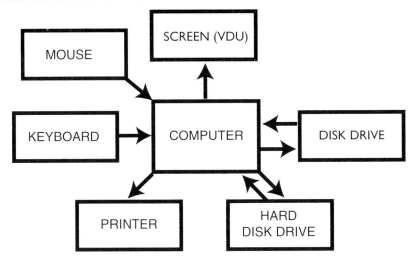

Figure 1.2 *Hardware diagram.*

We will now look at each part of the computer system in more detail.

The computer

The type of computer which you will use is a micro-computer. It is quite small and fits easily on a desk. Even smaller versions can be carried around and operated using rechargeable batteries. These are called lap-top computers.

Desk top and lap-top computers.

A mini computer used to control the flow of oil from field to refinery.

Although the processing power and speed of micro-computers has improved greatly over the last few years, they are not powerful enough or fast enough for all applications. Mini-computers are bigger machines and are much faster. They are used for many commercial applications. The traffic control system described in chapter 18 uses a mini-computer.

The largest computers are main-frame computers. These can process very large amounts of data extremely quickly.

A mainframe system.

In many commercial systems computers of different sizes are linked together. The supermarket system described in chapter 18 uses different sizes of computer at different levels in the organisation.

Inside the computer

Q

What are the main parts of the CPU? Give one function of each part.

The **central processing unit (CPU)** is sometimes described as the 'brain' of a computer system. This is where the instructions are actually carried out. Figure 1.3 shows the main parts of the CPU and the connections between them.

Each part of the CPU has its own job to do. The **control unit** controls movement of data inside the computer, and between the computer and the peripheral devices. It also looks after timing of operations. The **arithmetic and logic unit (ALU)** is where calculations are performed and logical comparisons are made. The

immediate access store (IAS) is the memory of the computer system, sometimes called **primary storage**. It is used to hold programs and data that are in use.

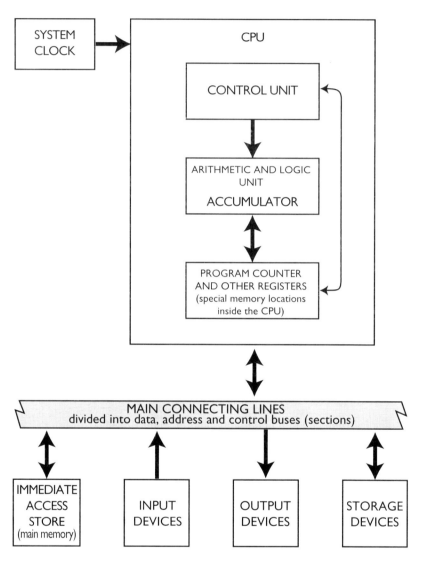

Figure 1.3 *CPU diagram.*

Q

Explain the differences between ROM and RAM.

Draw a block diagram to show the hardware needed for a computer system suitable for word processing. Explain why each part is needed.

There are two types of memory in a computer - **Read Only Memory (ROM)** and **Random Access Memory (RAM)**. The contents of ROM can't be altered by the user and the data in this type of memory is not lost when the computer is switched off. The contents of RAM can be changed by the user and this type of memory is used to hold the user's programs and data. The data in RAM is lost when the computer is switched off unless it has been saved on disk. RAM is described as **volatile memory** while ROM is **non-volatile memory**.

In the next three chapters we will look at some of the peripheral devices that can be attached to computers.

Input Devices

I nput devices are used to put data into a computer system. You can use some input devices, such as a **keyboard** or **mouse** to enter data by hand. Other input devices such as **bar code readers** allow **automated data entry** to take place. In this chapter we will look at some of the hand-operated devices and in chapter 3 we will look at some automated input devices.

Keyboards

An overlay keyboard.

A standard PC keyboard.

Q

Why might an overlay or touch-screen keyboard sometimes be used instead of a standard keyboard in each of these situations:

A fast food shop,

A public information system in a theme park?

K eyboards like the one in the photograph (above) are very widely used to put data into a computer system. You have probably used one to word-process some of your work. A standard computer keyboard has a layout similar to a typewriter keyboard, but with extra keys as well. The extra keys include function keys which can be used to start actions such as displaying help information. Their exact purpose is under the control of the software in use.

Although the standard keyboard is very useful for a wide range of applications there are some tasks for which it is not suitable.

Fast food shops use overlay keyboards like the one in the photograph (above left). These keyboards are fitted to the tills which are computer terminals. Each area on the keyboard represents one of the items sold. There are also numbers so that the operator can enter the number sold. The keyboard is flat and waterproof. This is very important as it makes it easy to clean and resistant to spills. An ordinary keyboard would be difficult to keep clean and a spilt drink would cause serious damage.

Mouse

A selection of computer mice.

A mouse, like the ones in the photograph (above), is a pointing device. You can use it to move a marker called a cursor around the screen. Underneath the mouse is a small ball. As you move the mouse on a flat surface, the ball rotates. This rotation is detected inside the mouse and data is transmitted to the computer. The software interprets this as directional data for moving the cursor.

Your mouse will also have at least two buttons on top of it. These are used to select items, start actions and cancel choices. Most software uses the left mouse button to select or start things and the right button to stop or cancel things.

A mouse is used when software provides pull down menus and buttons on the screen. Choices are made by moving the cursor with the mouse then clicking the mouse button. If you use a painting package then you will use a mouse for drawing. The movements you make with the mouse are converted to make a drawing on the screen.

Q

Why is a mouse called a pointing device?

Joy-stick

You may have used a joy-stick to play computer games. Like a mouse, it is used to input directional data. This data is then used by the game program to control movement of an object on the screen.

Graphics tablet or digitiser

A graphics tablet in use.

This device has a flat surface on which you can 'draw' using a special pen. As you draw, the pressure on the surface is detected and data about position (x and y coordinates) is sent to the computer. The main application for this device is to allow freehand drawings to be entered into the computer. Many people find this method much easier than using a mouse. You can see a graphics tablet in use in the photograph (left).

Scanner

A small, hand scanner in use.

You can use a scanner like the one shown in the photograph (above) to collect data about the light reflected by areas on a picture and transmit it to the computer. The scanning software builds up a digital image and displays the picture on the screen. Once you have scanned the picture you can edit the computer version, cut bits out of it, or rescale as required. Scanners can work in black, white and grey or they can work in colour. As you might expect, colour scanners are more expensive and the image files they produce take more storage space.

Scanners can also be used to input pages of text. Optical character reading software is needed to convert the graphics image of the text into a text file which can be edited using a word-processor. (See Chapter 3 for more on this topic.)

Video digitiser

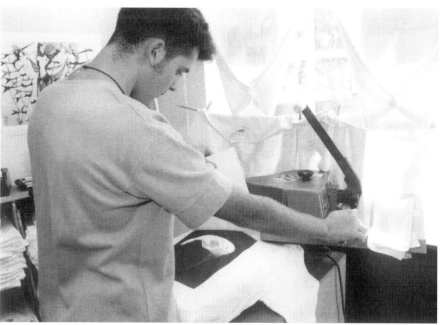

A video digitiser has been used to print this photograph on a T-shirt.

This is a device used to convert a video picture into a computer image. A video camera is used to produce a picture which is converted to a computer image and then sent to a printer to be put onto something. You can see a photograph of a flower being transferred onto a T-shirt in the picture (above). Once the image has been stored in a computer file it can be used in the same way as any other graphic.

3

Automated Input Devices

For some applications, vast amounts of data have to be input to the computer system. If this data was inputted using one of the manual methods it would either take a very long time or require a large number of data entry staff. Automated methods give fast data input and very few staff are needed.

There are several different automated methods and some are better than others for particular applications. As we look at each method we will also look at some of the applications for which it is used.

Optical Mark Recognition (OMR)

Q

What is OMR? Why is it used to input examination answers?

For this method the data is collected as marks made on preprinted forms like the one in Figure 3.1. This form is used for answering questions in multiple choice examinations. Each possible answer to every question has its own space on the form. The person doing the examination makes a dark pencil mark in the space for the answer he or she thinks is right. All the printing on the form is in very pale ink called fade-out ink. This ink is not detected by the reading machine.

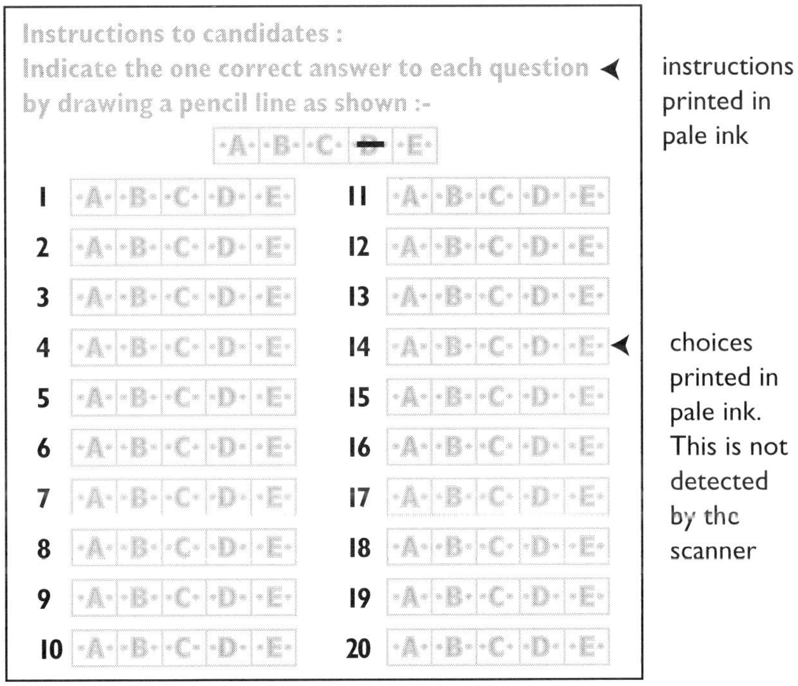

Figure 3.1 A multiple choice card used in exams.

instructions printed in pale ink

choices printed in pale ink. This is not detected by the scanner

At the end of the examination all the forms are collected together and put through an optical mark reader. This machine detects the amount of light reflected from different parts of the form. The dark marks reflect less light. The machine transmits data about each space to the computer and the software works out whether the answers are right or wrong and adds up the total mark.

Sometimes the forms won't go through the machine because they have been creased. Other forms can't be read because they have got dirty or marks have been made in the wrong place. The data from these rejected forms has to be entered by hand.

OMR is also used for entering numeric data. National Lottery choices are entered using this method and some gas and electricity boards use it to enter meter readings. This method is fast compared with manual methods and, provided the person filling in the form is careful, it is accurate with a very low level of read errors.

Optical Character Recognition (OCR)

Q

Why is OCR not usually used to input handwritten text?

A page being read by OCR.

An optical character reader also works by detecting the amount of light reflected from a sheet of paper. Data about the pattern of light and dark areas on the paper is transmitted to the computer. This pattern of data is compared with stored patterns for different characters. The best match is selected and the code representing this character is stored.

OCR has improved considerably in the last few years. It used to be slow with a high percentage of errors in reading, and only a few kinds of print could be read. Now reading is quicker, most standard fonts can be recognised and the number of reading errors is much lower.

Magnetic Ink Character Recognition (MICR)

This method of data input is used in banking (see Chapter 15). The data to be input is printed onto cheques in a special ink. This ink can be magnetised by the reading machine and the pattern of magnetisation is recognised. One standard character set is used. This contains very few characters so comparisons are done quickly and reading is very fast.

MICR provides accurate reading and a high level of security. Simple alteration or overwriting of the data using ordinary inks will not affect reading. MICR is fairly expensive and therefore is not used in other applications.

MICR is used in banks for entering data from cheques. Why can't OCR be used for this application?

Some of the data on the cheque, such as the bank's sorting code, the account number and the cheque number, are printed before the cheque book is sent to the customer. You can see these in the photograph (below). The amount has to be added later, before the cheque goes into the reading machine.

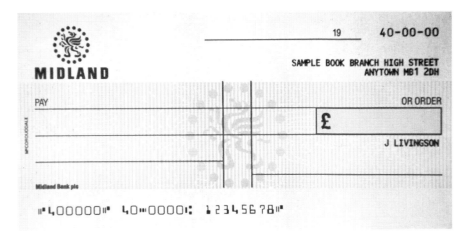

A cheque showing pre-printed data.

Bar code readers

Bar codes like the one in Figure 3.2 are read by a bar code scanner.

A bar code being scanned.

The amount of light reflected by the dark and light lines in the bar code is detected by the reader. Different widths of dark and light bars represent different characters. The bar code has separate left and right halves and can be read in either direction.

The bar code represents a number. This number is the data which is input to the computer system. Bar codes are used in supermarket systems (see Chapter 18) and they are also used in many libraries.

Figure 3.2 A bar code.

In a library each book has a printed bar code label stuck in it or on its cover. The borrower's ticket also has a bar code. This allows data about loans and returns of books to be entered into the library computer system quickly and with greater accuracy than by entering numbers on a keyboard.

Q

List three different applications where bar codes could be used to input data.

It is possible for the reading machine to misread a bar code. For example, there might be frost on a bag of peas, or the bar code might have a dirty mark on it. The bar code contains a check digit to make sure that the number read is valid. This is a single figure worked out from all the other figures in the code by doing a series of calculations. This digit is attached to the rest of the bar code when it is printed. When the code is read, the check digit is recalculated and the answer is compared with the check digit read from the printed bar code. If the two figures are the same then the code has been read properly and the data is valid. If they are not the same then the code must be scanned again. The scanning system usually beeps when a code is accepted and stays quiet if it is read wrongly. Data is only accepted when a beep sounds. If the code will not scan after a few attempts then the code number can be typed in using a keyboard. You will find out more about bar codes in the section on supermarket systems in chapter 18.

Magnetic strip codes

Strips of magnetisable material can be built into plastic cards, as in the photograph (below), and these strips can be magnetised to store data. They are used on credit cards and bank cards and the data they store is usually the account number and expiry date of the card. The amount of data which can be stored is limited to about 70 characters, so there isn't room for very much data.

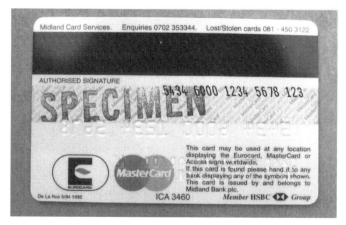

The back of a credit card showing the magnetic strip.

Q

What data does the magnetic strip on a credit card hold?

The card is passed through a reading machine and the pattern of magnetisation is detected and converted to numeric data. Reading is rapid and accurate. Check digits are used for validation as with bar codes. These cards work well but they can be easily damaged. The magnetic pattern which represents the data can be altered if the card is exposed to a strong magnet. If this happens the card will no longer be readable by the machine and the numbers have to be typed in by hand. This kind of damage is quite common and can be caused by the magnets used to remove security tags in shops.

◼ *Smart cards*

Q

What is the difference between a magnetic strip card and a smart card?

Suggest three applications for which smart cards could be used.

A smart card is different from a magnetic strip card although they may look rather similar. A smart card can have data written to it after the card has been produced because it contains memory circuits. It can hold much more data than a magnetic strip card and the data can be changed. This type of card is likely to be more widely used in the future and will probably replace the magnetic strip credit cards used at present. Petrol companies are using smart cards, like the ones in the photograph (below), to store data about 'points' which are added when the card owner buys some petrol. When points are used to pay for something, the data on the card is changed to delete the used points.

Smart cards used for petrol points and air miles.

Smart cards can also be used to operate a toll system on motorways, or at bridges and tunnels. The card has a certain number of units written into its memory when the card is purchased. It is put into a holder on the windscreen of the car and units are cancelled as it goes past the toll point. This avoids the delays which are caused when drivers have to stop to pay the toll.

Kimball tags

This method of data input is still used by some clothes shops. The tag is a small piece of card with holes punched in it to represent the data. The card can hold a small amount of data and will contain a code for the item, and sometimes a branch or department code as well. Extra information can be printed on the card so that customers can read it. The price and size are usually printed on the card. The tags are attached to the garments and when they are sold the tag is removed. All the tags are kept together and at the end of the day they are fed into a reading machine which detects the pattern of holes and converts this to a number. This data is used to update the stock files and to order new stock. The use of Kimball tags is declining as more and more shops switch to magnetic strip coding or bar codes on garment labels. Both of these methods have the advantage of working with Point of Sale (POS) systems which immediately update the stock files. This is not possible with Kimball tags as they are always processed as a batch.

Sensors

Sensors can be used to detect external changes such as variations in heat, light and pressure. Data from the sensors is converted to digital values and transmitted to the computer system. It can be processed immediately to influence outputs from the computer system or it can be stored on disk or tape to be analysed later. The traffic control computer system described in Chapter 18 receives data from sensors and so does the computer system used to control freezer and chiller temperatures in the supermarket (Chapter 18).

4 Storage of Data on Disks

Why is data stored?

Data put into computer systems has to be transferred to **backing store** so that it will not be lost when the computer system is switched off. Backing store is the general name given to disks and tape used to store data. **Storage devices** allow data to be saved on a suitable **medium** so that it can be reused. The medium is the **disk** or **tape** on which the data is stored. The storage device is the **disk drive** or **tape drive** which reads and writes the data.

Magnetic disks and tapes are still the commonest storage media but **optical disks** and **magneto-optical disks** are being used more and more.

Before we can really understand storage properly we need to know something about data and how quantities of data are measured.

Data

A computer works with data and this is stored as **binary numbers**. A binary number consists of the digits 0 and 1 only. This is a binary number:

01011101

A single binary digit needs one **bit** of storage in the computer memory or on backing store. Eight bits make up one **byte** and this is enough storage space for a single character. To store the character A we need space for the binary code which represents this letter. The code is 01000001 and it needs eight bits or one byte of storage.

A **kilobyte** (K) is 1024 bytes. This might seem like an odd number to choose but it is actually 2^{10} bytes. (Remember that the computer works in binary which is base 2 arithmetic.) A **megabyte** (Mb) is 1000 kilobytes. This is approximately 1 million bytes. A **gigabyte** (Gb) is 1000 megabytes. These units of memory are used when describing the storage capacity of disks and tapes.

Q

What is

a bit
a byte
a megabyte?

Magnetic disks

All magnetic disks hold data as magnetised spots on the disk surface. The data is stored by magnetising the spot in one direction to represent a binary 1 and in a different direction to represent a binary 0. Each bit is stored separately and the data is arranged in circular **tracks** on the disk surface. The tracks are divided into **sectors** as shown in Figure 4.1.

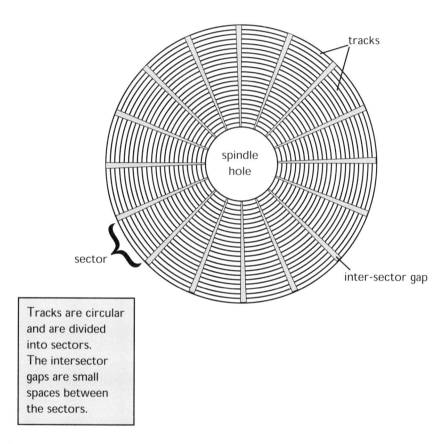

Tracks are circular
and are divided
into sectors.
The intersector
gaps are small
spaces between
the sectors.

Figure 4.1 *Layout of data on a magnetic disk.*

If both sides of the disk are used then the tracks in the same place on the two sides form a cylinder. Data is written to and read from the disk in blocks, and a block of data fits into a sector on the disk surface. Each data block can be accessed by supplying its cylinder and sector number. This kind of access to data is called **direct access** because other tracks and sectors on the disk are not read first.

Hard disks, like the one in the photograph (opposite, top), are made of metal coated with a magnetisable material. They can hold a large amount of data and they are usually fixed inside the hard disk drive. The heads which move across the disk to read and write the data are extremely close to the surface and a speck of dust can easily cause damage. Sealing the disk inside the disk drive keeps it clean.

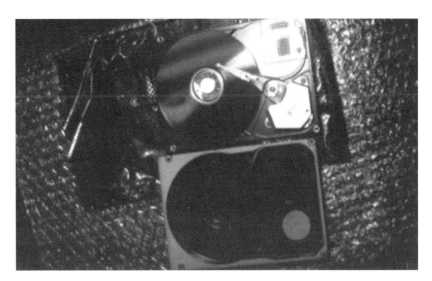

The inside of a hard drive.

As well as giving a large amount of storage space on the disk, a hard disk drive accesses data (reads it) much faster than a floppy disk drive. This is important because modern software often needs to move data to and from the hard disk. It doesn't keep everything in memory all the time. If the disk drive has a slow **access time** then it will make the software run slowly, even if the computer has a fast processor.

Floppy disks are made of plastic coated with a magnetisable material. They are sealed into a protective case which has openings to allow data to be written and read. The case can be made of card but the most commonly used disks have rigid plastic cases. The disks come in different sizes and the size has to be right for the disk drive. The size most commonly used is 3.5 inches. You can see a variety of floppy disks in the photograph (left).

A floppy disk holds up to 1.44 Mb of data. This is not very much compared to the size of many applications packages and these are supplied on several floppy disks. All the disks for one package can be seen in the photograph (below).

Floppy disks come in various sizes.

The distribution disks for one software package.

Floppy disks have to be used for supplying software to users but it is rare for programs to be run from the floppy disks. They are usually installed on the hard disk before they will run. Floppy disks are also useful for keeping data files, providing these are not too big. They are also used to hold back-up copies of the data and programs on the hard disk.

Optical disks (CD-ROMS) look like the compact disks used for music and they work in the same way. Data is stored by changing the way the surface reflects a low energy laser beam. The light is reflected differently depending on whether the bit stored is a 1 or a 0. A low intensity beam is used to read the data but a higher intensity beam is needed to write the data onto the disk.

Once the surface has been altered to store data it can't be changed so optical disks can only be written once, although they can be read many times. For this reason they cannot be used for all applications.

Optical disks can hold a lot of data, approximately 512 megabytes, so a single CD-ROM can hold a whole encyclopaedia, and also the software needed to look things up easily. CD-ROMs are exchangeable, unlike most hard disks, and software producers are beginning to supply packages on CD-ROM, instead of on lots of floppy disks. This has advantages for both the supplier and the user of the software:

- CD-ROMS are more reliable than floppy disks so there should be no problems with media.

- The software will sometimes run from the CD-ROM and need not be installed onto the hard disk.

- Software doesn't need to be copied for back-up purposes and software theft is less likely to happen.

- Programs can be bigger and more support files such as clip-art can be supplied.

CD-ROM is no use if data files need to be changed and an alternative called magneto-optical disk has been developed. This uses both optical and magnetic methods of storage. Data is stored using optical methods then, if the data needs to be changed, magnetic storage is used to store the change. These drives can be used in the same way as hard disk drives but have the advantage of using exchangeable disks with high capacity.

Q

Give one advantage and one disadvantage of CD-ROM as a storage medium.

Storing Data on Tape

M agnetic tape can be used to store data but it is not suitable for all applications. Reel-to-reel tape is used mainly in large computer systems handling vast amounts of data which is processed in the order it was stored. You can see an example in the photograph (below).

A reel-to-reel tape drive in a main-frame computer.

Magnetic tape and containers.

Q

Why is magnetic tape not suitable for all applications?

One of the limitations of tape as a storage medium is that the data stored on it has to be read from the beginning even if the piece of data needed is right at the end. It is described as a **serial access** medium. This kind of medium is suitable for applications where all, or most, of the records need to be processed and can be dealt with in the order in which they are stored. An example of this kind of application is processing payments of employees of a large firm. Everyone working for the firm will have to be paid so all records will need to be processed. The firm will have to pay everyone at the same time so it will be convenient to do the processing in one big batch.

The tape used is stored on reels and these fit into large tape drives. The tapes can be swapped over and each tape is very long (2400 feet) so they hold lots of data. When a tape is not in use it is kept in a plastic container. You can see tapes and their containers in the photograph (above left).

Data is always arranged in the same way on a tape. The **bits** of data representing a character are stored in a frame across the tape as in Figure 5.1. There is a separate track on the tape for each data bit and also an extra **parity track**. This track can be used to store **parity bits**, which are used to carry out a validation check when data is read from the tape. A **validation check** makes sure that the data read is sensible and reasonable. (You can find out more about validation checks in chapter 7.)

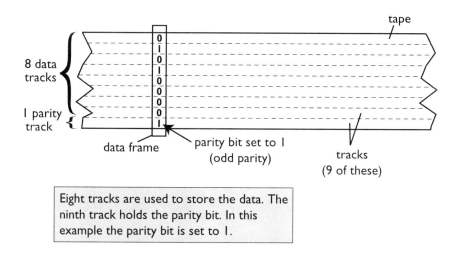

Eight tracks are used to store the data. The ninth track holds the parity bit. In this example the parity bit is set to 1.

Figure 5.1 Diagram of a data frame.

Q

Explain how data is arranged on magnetic tape.

The data is organised into blocks with interblock gaps between them. A block can often hold several records and there will be end-of-record markers between the records. A block is the amount of data which is read or written at one time. The interblock gaps allow for starting and stopping of the tape in the tape drive (see Figure 5.2).

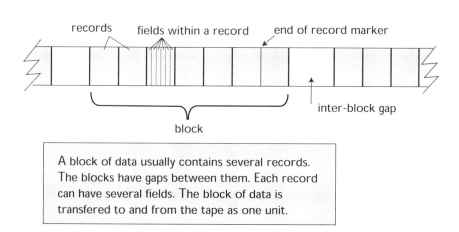

A block of data usually contains several records. The blocks have gaps between them. Each record can have several fields. The block of data is transfered to and from the tape as one unit.

Tape is very useful for keeping back-up copies of data. A **tape**

Figure 5.2 Diagram to show the layout of data on magnetic tape.

Q

What is a tape streamer?
What is it used for?

Tape is very useful for keeping back-up copies of data. A **tape streamer**, like the one in the photograph (below), holds a small tape cartridge and this can be used to make a back-up copy of all the data stored on a hard disk. If anything goes wrong with the hard disk then the copy on the tape cartridge can be used to replace the lost data.

Reel to reel magnetic tape is often used to store all the details of

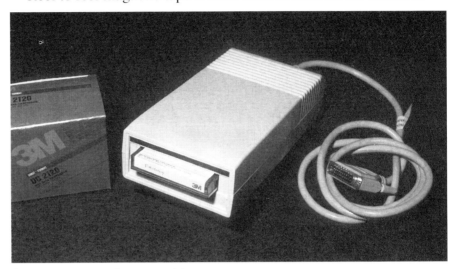

A tape streamer and tape cartridges.

changes made to files on disk. In an airline booking system the main files will be copied from magnetic disk to tape at least once a day. This back-up tape will be stored safely. The main files on magnetic disk will be changed during the day as seats on a plane are reserved. At the same time as the file on disk is altered, a record is stored on a magnetic tape as well. This tape contains the **transaction log file**. If data is lost from the disk then this tape can be used together with the last daily back-up tape to restore the lost data on disk. The only data which is totally lost will be data concerning the change being made when the system failed.

Magnetic tape can hold a lot of data and the data can be transferred to and from the tape very rapidly. If an application uses only serial access it makes sense to store the data on tape. Back up copies are always read from beginning to end so tape is ideal for this purpose as it is the cheapest way of storing the quantities of data involved.

Q

Give one advantage of using magnetic tape rather than a magnetic disk for storing data.

6

Output Devices

T hese devices are used to get information out of the computer system in a form which the user can understand. During output the data will be put into a context so that it becomes information. The display screen or VDU and printers are examples of output devices. We will look at a range of different devices in this chapter, concentrating on what each device can do rather than how it works.

▮ *Display screens (VDUs)*

E very desk-top computer has a display screen of some kind. This is often called the **monitor**. The screens are available in a range of sizes, and screen size is measured diagonally from the top left corner to the bottom right corner. A screen display can be either monochrome or colour. Monochrome screens are not necessarily black and white, they can have green or orange text on a black background instead. If a computer system will only ever be used to handle text displays then a monochrome display will be suitable. Monochrome monitors are cheaper and smaller than colour monitors. You can see a selection of different monitors in the photograph (below).

A selection of monitors.

Q

What is meant by screen resolution? Why is it important?

The **resolution** of the monitor is very important. This is the number of separate points across and down the screen which can be displayed. For some applications, such as design work using CAD packages, it is essential to have an extremely high resolution. If the resolution is not high enough then the lines in the drawing will not be clear. Desk-top publishing also needs a reasonably high screen resolution (see the photograph below). It is possible to produce a screen image which apparently has a higher resolution than the screen can display. This is done by a method called interlacing. It produces more screen flicker than a non-interlaced display.

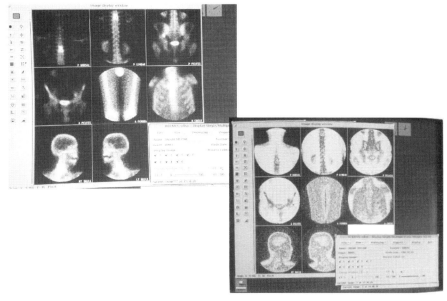

The same images on medium and high resolution screens.

The screen image is made up of little squares called **pixels**. If there are not many squares then the image will have lines with jagged edges. More squares gives a smoother-looking line (see Figure 6.1).

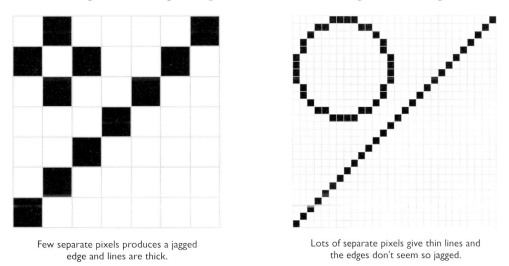

Few separate pixels produces a jagged edge and lines are thick.

Lots of separate pixels give thin lines and the edges don't seem so jagged.

Figure 6.1 *Diagram to show lines made from different sized blocks.*

A lap-top showing the screen display.

Desk-top displays use monitors which work in the same way as a television set but these are far too bulky to be used with portable lap-top computers. Lap-tops need a flat screen. The screen on a lap-top computer can be monochrome or colour but monochrome is commonest. You can seen an example of a lap-top screen in the photograph (left). The way in which the screen works is completely different from a standard VDU and more like the way in which a calculator display operates. This can make the screen difficult to read unless it has its own light behind it. Lap-top screens can have the same resolution as desk-top screens.

Printers

A huge variety of printers is available and choosing the best one for a particular system is not always easy. Different kinds of printer produce different qualities of output and speed of output also varies. Running costs vary for different types of printer and this may be important as well. We will look at a range of types of printer and their particular strengths and weaknesses.

Impact printers produce their output by hammering pins or character patterns against a ribbon and the paper. This means that all of them are noisy when they are working. There are three main types.

The **dot matrix printer**, like the one in the photograph (below), uses **pins** to build up the characters or drawings as a series of dots. A printer with nine pins makes less dots than a printer with 24 pins so the output it produces is not as good. These printers have the advantage of being cheap to buy and to run. The ribbons they use are not expensive and they print on **continuous paper** or on separate sheets of ordinary paper. Some dot matrix printers can produce colour using a multi-coloured ribbon. The main disadvantages are the noise, the slow speed, and the rather poor quality of output of nine-pin printers.

A dot matrix printer.

Q

What are the advantages of a line printer? Suggest two applications for which a line printer would be suitable.

Line printers are also impact printers. They produce their output a whole line at a time by hammering character patterns against the ribbon and paper. They are fast printers and are ideal for situations where lots of output is needed quickly and the quality is not particularly important. They use continuous paper and have a low running cost. They are very noisy and they can't produce graphics. You can see one illustrated in the photograph (below).

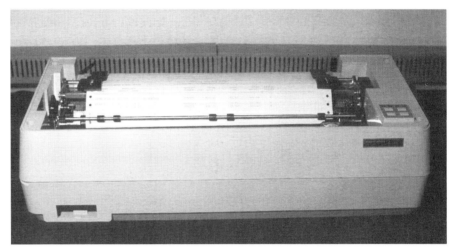

A line printer.

Daisy wheel printers (see the photograph below) are still in use in some offices. They hammer character patterns against a ribbon and the paper and produce a high quality output. They are noisy and they can only produce the kinds of characters included on the particular daisy wheel in use, although the wheels can be changed. Their output is very slow compared with other printers and they can't produce graphics.

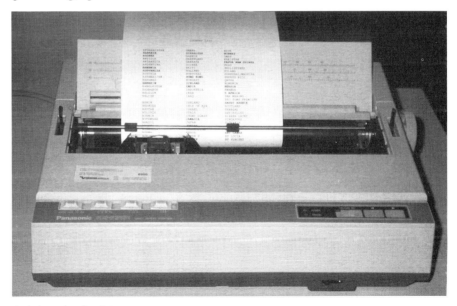

A daisy wheel printer.

Non-impact printers are quiet when working and produce high quality output. They can all produce graphics and most types are capable of producing colour. Each type produces its output in a different way.

A **laser printer**, illustrated below, uses a laser beam to build up an electrical image of a page on a light-sensitive drum in the same way as a photocopier. The image is built up from dots, but with at least 300 dots to an inch the individual dots can't be seen. Once the image has been formed on the drum a powder called **toner** is held against the paper in the same pattern. The paper and toner is then heated to fix the powder to the paper. Laser printers use ordinary paper and are quite fast. Speeds are measured in pages per minute and a fast printer can produce over 20 pages per minute. The output is of very high quality and graphics can be produced. The main disadvantage is cost. The printer is quite expensive to buy, especially if colour is needed, and running costs are higher than for impact printers.

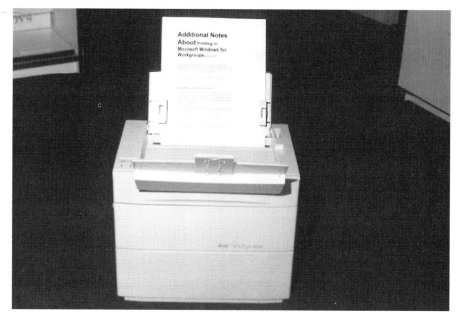

A laser printer.

Ink-jet printers produce their output by spraying tiny drops of ink onto the paper. They make up the image from dots using 300 or 450 dots to an inch. This gives a high quality output. They can work in black or in colour. They use ordinary paper but won't work very well if the paper is too absorbent because the wet ink tends to spread before it dries. They are slower than laser printers but are cheaper to buy. Running costs for black output are about the same. They can print graphics. You can see an ink-jet printer in the photograph (opposite, top).

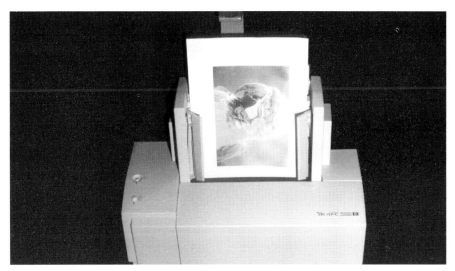

An ink jet printer.

Thermal printers use special heat sensitive paper and produce their output by heating spots on the paper to make it go black. Output is of fairly high quality and the main disadvantage is the need for thermal paper. It's possible to produce graphic output using this type of printer (see the photograph below).

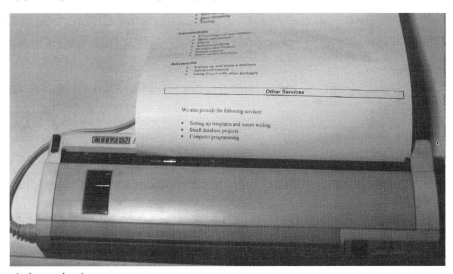

A thermal printer.

Q

What advantages does a plotter have compared with a printer for producing accurate drawings?

When large drawings have to be produced, for example designs for a car, the best output device is a **plotter**, which you can see in the photograph overleaf. These come in sizes matching the standard sizes of paper and they can be very large. The drawing is produced using pens and the drawing pen can reach any point on the piece of paper. The lines drawn are continuous, they are not made of dots, and the drawing produced is very accurate. Output is quite slow but, when plotters are used, the speed is much less important than accuracy. Colour can be included in the drawing as the plotter can change its pen automatically.

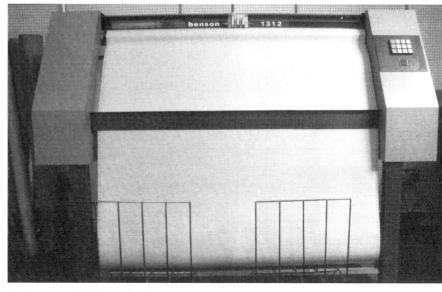

A plotter producing a drawing.

A microfiche and a reader.

What is microfiche? Give one application for which it is used.

Output on microfiche

This device is used when large volumes of data (usually text) have to be stored in a human-readable form. The output is a reduced size transparency of each page, with 50 pages on a single **microfiche**. The microfiche has to be magnified in order to read it so a special reading machine has to be available, which can be seen left. Lists of all books in print are available in this form.

Output of sound

Speakers are used to output sound. They are the same as the speakers used with music systems. Computer systems used to run multimedia software are often supplied with the speakers built into the computer case. On other systems the speakers are connected by cables to special hardware fitted inside the case. With a good speaker system the computer can output high quality sound.

Control of other devices

Output can be used to control devices such as robots and lathes. The computer output operates parts such as switches and hydraulic systems in these devices.

CHAPTER

7

The Operating System and System Software

In this chapter we will look at the software which controls the operation of the computer hardware. The **operating system** is a program which manages all the resources of the computer system. All operating systems have to be able to carry out certain tasks.

The operating system allocates memory for storing programs and data so that when data is needed it can be found easily. New data is not put in areas of memory which have already been allocated.

The operating system has routines for handling input and output operations. It accepts data from input devices, transferring this data to memory, and it retrieves data from memory and sends it to output devices. This is not quite so simple as it sounds. There may be more than one input device and the operating system has to find out that a device has data to send, and then handle the data in the correct way. Data coming in from the keyboard is handled differently from data coming from a mouse. The operating system has to use the correct routines to handle each device.

When the operating system is sending data to output devices it has to ensure that the data goes to the correct device. Data intended for the printer must not end up on the screen instead.

The operating system also has to be able to look after data storage in the computer system's memory. It needs to keep track of what space is available and what has already been allocated.

The operating system looks after transfers of data between the backing store and memory. If a file has to be read from disk, operating system routines are needed to open the file and to transfer the blocks of data. To do this it has to be able to find the file first. The operating system has a specific search path which it uses when looking for a file on the disk. If a file is being written to disk then the operating system builds up blocks until they are ready for transfer. As each block is ready it is sent to the disk drive which writes it onto the disk.

We can sum up the functions of the operating system by saying that it provides the routines needed to allow application software to interact with the hardware.

Q

Describe three functions of all operating systems.

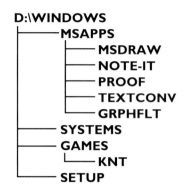

```
D:\WINDOWS
├───────MSAPPS
│         ├──────MSDRAW
│         ├──────NOTE-IT
│         ├──────PROOF
│         ├──────TEXTCONV
│         └──────GRPHFLT
├───────SYSTEMS
├───────GAMES
│         └──────KNT
└───────SETUP
```

Figure 7.1 Structure of a hard disk directory.

What is a sub-directory? Why are sub-directories used?

What is a batch file? Why are batch files used?

System commands

Operating systems have their own **commands**. We can use operating system commands to find out what is on a disk by displaying the **disk directory**. Hard disks can holds lots of data so the disk directory is usually divided up into **subdirectories** and these can have subdirectories as well. The operating system commands let us create and remove subdirectories so that we can organise the disk storage sensibly. Figure 7.1 shows an example of the organisation of a disk directory. It is a bit like a **tree** with lots of branches.

Finding things on a hard disk would take a long time if the whole of every directory had to be examined, so the operating system lets us set up **search paths**. It uses the path to look for the files which are needed. To find a file in the subdirectory 'proof' in the example (left) we need to use the path

D:\windows\msapps\proof

We can put together **batches** of commands to carry out particular tasks. A particular package may use its own subdirectory so we can put together a batch of commands to switch to this directory and to load the package. These commands can be saved with a name and this name can then be used just like a system command word to make the package load. These **batch files** (see Figure 7.2) are often produced when a new package is installed on the computer system.

This file creates a new sub-directory from the root directory of drive C. It then copies all the files from the floppy disk in drive A into the new sub-directory. The echo commands display screen messages.

```
echo off
echo Installing software to drive C
echo A new sub-directory from the root directory will be created.
echo All the picture files will then be copied into this directory.
cd\
md\pictures
copy a:*.*c:\pictures
echo Installation complete
```

Figure 7.2 Example of a batch file.

As well as the operating system itself, a computer system is supplied with various **system utility programs**. These are designed to do some of the routine jobs, like **formatting** floppy disks, by writing track and sector data on them. Disks can't be used until they have been formatted. Utilities can also check disks for **bad sectors** which can't store data. There are also utilities for copying files from one disk to another and for sorting files and printing them.

The operating system will not always manage new devices properly. If a new and complicated printer is added to the system then extra software will need to be added to make the printer work. This kind of software is called a **device driver**. Once it is installed on the hard disk, the data going to the printer will be processed by the device driver software before being sent to the printer by the operating system output routine.

Different kinds of operating system

Different kinds of operating system are needed for various kinds of computer. As the operating system works directly with the hardware it is understandable that different hardware will need different commands to make the same thing happen.

A more complicated kind of operating system is needed to run computers which are shared by lots of users, each with a different terminal. A diagram of how it works is shown in Figure 7.3. This kind of system needs to be able to keep the programs and data belonging to the various users completely separate. It also needs to be able to store data going to the printer in a **print queue** so that output from different users doesn't get mixed up. It will have to ensure that each user gets a fair share of processor time without any long delays. This is done by switching very rapidly between terminals. Each terminal that needs processor time gets a fraction of a second in turn. This may not seem very long but a lot can be done as the computer can process millions of instructions every second. **Multi-user** systems like this are based around large, fast computers.

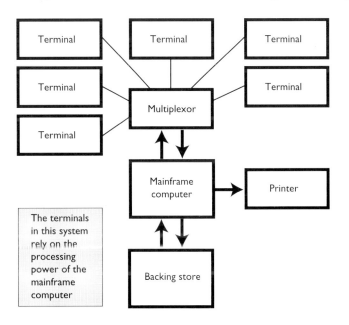

The terminals in this system rely on the processing power of the mainframe computer

Figure 7.3 Diagram of a multi-user system.

Q

In a multi-user system each user seems to be able to use the CPU at the same time. How is this achieved?

In a multi-programming system how does the operating system make sure that the different programs and data don't get mixed up?

There are also systems which seem to run more than one program at once. They do this by switching between the programs. These systems are called **multi-programming systems**. The operating system has to be able to keep all the programs and their data in separate areas of memory, so memory management is more complicated. You can see how this works in Figure 7.4.

The various jobs that the system is doing at one time have to be given priorities so that the best possible use is made of all the system resources. The operating system has to be able to use these priorities when switching between jobs. Multi-programming operating systems are, therefore, very complex.

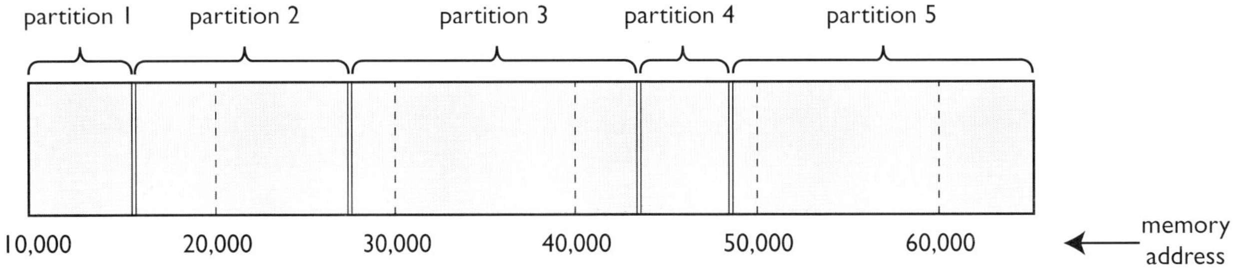

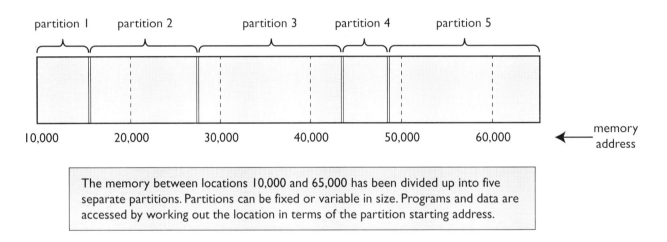

The memory between locations 10,000 and 65,000 has been divided up into five separate partitions. Partitions can be fixed or variable in size. Programs and data are accessed by working out the location in terms of the partition starting address.

Figure 7.4 *How memory partitioning works.*

CHAPTER

8

Organising Data for Storage

All data is stored in **files** which have to have file names. Data in a file is divided into **records** which can have a very simple structure. In some files it may contain just one piece of data. In this case the record has a single **field**. In data files created by a user with a database package, the record structure tends to be much more complex. The records in these files contain many different fields and each field contains one item of data. You can see how all these elements are related in Figure 8.1.

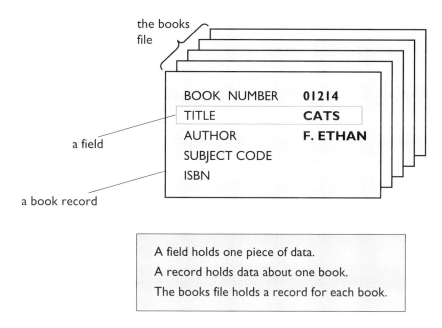

the books file

a field

a book record

BOOK NUMBER	01214
TITLE	CATS
AUTHOR	F. ETHAN
SUBJECT CODE	
ISBN	

A field holds one piece of data.

A record holds data about one book.

The books file holds a record for each book.

Figure 8.1 *Files, records and fields.*

Text files

A simple text file consists of the code (**ASCII** character code) for each character in the file. End of line markers have their own ASCII code so they are included. This kind of file is very useful when moving text files between different word processing packages because it does not contain any special command or formatting codes.

Q

What is

a file
a record
a field?

33

A picture on the computer screen can be stored in a graphics file.

Graphics files

These files have to contain lots of data. There are several ways of organising the data; these are called **file formats**. One of these is the **bit-mapped format**. In this kind of file, data is stored about the colour of each pixel to be displayed on the screen.

For a particular image size, the file size will always be the same because there will be the same number of pixels on the screen.

Other types of graphics file store details of the **objects** which make up the picture. This takes less space because data isn't needed about every pixel on the screen. Both types of file need to contain data about the exact colours used to make the picture. The set of colours is called the **palette**.

Q

Why are graphics files sometimes very big?

Why are different types of files needed?

Database file and record structures

When you set up a database you create your own data files and your own records. You can have one file or more than one. Files are sometimes called **data tables**. A file contains all the data about one topic and it has its own record structure. To set up a library database system, one of the files we need contains data about all the books in the library. A record in this file contains data about one book. All the records in the file have the same structure because we need to store the same sort of data about each book. We could use these fields:

> Book_number
> Title
> Author
> Subject_code
> ISBN

Each record has to have one field that will contain a value which will never be repeated in another record. This is the book number and each book has its own unique number. The book_number field is called the **primary key field** for this file.

The fields can be of a fixed length or they can vary in length in different records. Fixed length fields make it easy to allocate space for records on backing store but they can waste quite a lot of storage space because the length has to be made big enough to hold the largest possible data item. In the books file we would need to allow quite a lot of space for the title because some books have very long names. In records for books with short names the spare part of the field is filled with spaces. You can see an example of this in Figure 8.2.

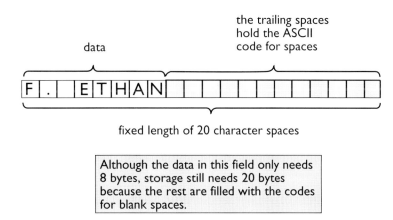

data   the trailing spaces
hold the ASCII
code for spaces

fixed length of 20 character spaces

Although the data in this field only needs
8 bytes, storage still needs 20 bytes
because the rest are filled with the codes
for blank spaces.

Figure 8.2 *Fixed length field showing packing with blanks.*

What are the advantages and disadvantages of fixed length and variable length fields?

Variable length fields save space on backing store because each data item gets just the right amount of space. At the end of the field there has to be an **end-of-field marker** to show where data for the field stops. Problems can arise if a short record is edited and becomes longer, because it won't go back into the same storage space as before. A new place has to be found for it on the backing store and the old space is used to hold data about where the record is located now. When this happens to lots of records it slows down searching of the data. For this reason database files usually use fixed length records.

Variable length records work well if all the records in a file are changed in one batch and the file is handled in the order it was created in, because a new version of the file can be made. (See Chapter 9.)

Using more than one data file

What is a relational database management system?

Why is data sometimes stored using several separate data tables rather than one large file?

For some applications it makes sense to organise the data into two or more files so that there is very little duplication of data, and the data that is stored can be used in more ways. A **Relational Database Management System** lets us do this. We will look at how we might organise the data for a library system.

A library system needs to store more than just the details of the books in the library. It needs details of the people who are members of the library as well. It also needs to store details of who has borrowed books. We have to have a members file with a record for each member, a books file with a record for each book, and a loans file with a record for each book on loan. You can see the fields for each of these files in Figure 8.3.

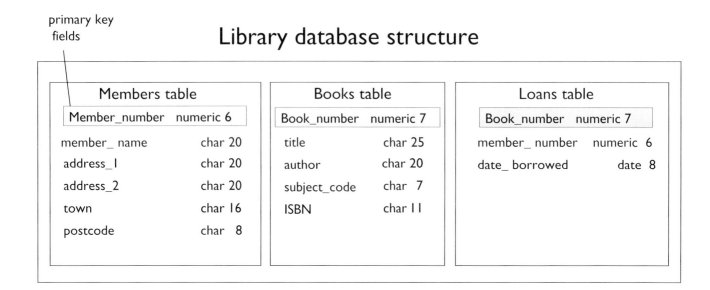

primary key
fields

Library database structure

Members table

Member_number	numeric 6
member_ name	char 20
address_1	char 20
address_2	char 20
town	char 16
postcode	char 8

Books table

Book_number	numeric 7
title	char 25
author	char 20
subject_code	char 7
ISBN	char 11

Loans table

Book_number	numeric 7
member_ number	numeric 6
date_ borrowed	date 8

Each table has a primary key field. This field will contain a unique value for each record so, by searching the contents of the primary key field, users can find any single record.

Figure 8.3 Database structures for a library system.

The members file contains all the data a member has to supply when they join the library. The primary key field is the member_number field. The books file contains all the data about each book the library owns. The primary key field in this case is the book_number field. The loans file has just three fields: book_number, member_number and date_borrowed. This means that when a book is borrowed very little data has to be entered, so people don't have to wait a long time when they want to take out a book. Every time a book is borrowed a new record will be created in this file. When a book is returned, the loan record for that book will be deleted.

Sometimes people don't bring books back when they should. The library system must be able to print out reminders to send to these people. Assuming that books are lent for four weeks, we need to find records in the loans file in which the date_borrowed is more than four weeks ago. We would then use the member_number to look up the member's name and address in the members file. We need to tell the member which book we want back so we have to use the book_number to look up the title and author in the books file.

We do all this by linking the records in the loans file to records in the members and books files. Figure 8.4 shows the links we have to make.

The lines in the diagram show whether there will be one or more records in a file to which the linked fields will match. The file used as the starting point for the search is called the 'parent' file and the linked file is called the 'child' file.

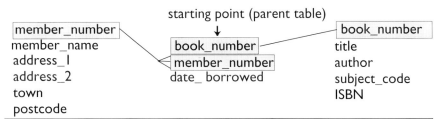

Each record in the loans file will link to one record in the books file. There may be more than one record in the loans file linking to the same member record, because a member can borrow more than one book.

Figure 8.4 Links between the library files.

What types of links can be made between data tables?

The links can be one-to-one, one-to-many, or many-to-one. In a one-to-one link, each record in the parent file will have one matching record in the child file. The link between the loans file and the books file is this kind of link because a book can only be borrowed by one person at a time.

In a one-to-many link there can be more than one matching record in the child file for each record in the parent file.

When the link is many-to-one there can be many records in the parent file which link to one record in the child file. The link between the loans file and the members file is of this type because one member can borrow more than one book, and each book would have its own loans record, all linking to the same member record.

This kind of organisation allows great flexibility in retrieving information. We can start from any of the files and combine data held in different files. We have very little duplication of data, just member_number and book_number occur twice each. If we used one big file we would need to store all the member details in the book record every time a book was borrowed. If a member borrowed four books this data would be stored four times. It would also take much longer to process loans because all this data would have to be entered into the system.

Checking data

What is verification? Why is it important that data is verified?

When data is entered into a computer system it has to be checked. There are two kinds of checking that can be carried out. A **verification check** is designed to make sure that data entered, or transferred from one medium to another, has been copied accurately. There are various ways of verifying data on input or transfer. When data is entered at a keyboard, verification is often achieved by having the data typed in twice by different operators. The two versions are compared and, if they match, the data is stored. If the two versions don't match the mistake has to be found by referring to the data collection sheet (the source document). The mistake can then be corrected and the data can be stored.

Q

What is validation? Give three examples of validation checks.

A very simple way of trying to verify input data is to display it on the screen and ask if it is correct. The user has to press the 'Y' key or click on a box to confirm that the data is what it should be. The problem with this method of verifying data is that users quite often assume they've typed everything in correctly and don't read the screen before pressing 'Y' or the mouse button.

The other kind of check is a **validation check**. This is carried out by the software to make sure that the data is sensible and that it won't cause problems when it is processed. There are different kinds of validation check to detect different types of error.

Type checks are used to make sure that numerical data doesn't accidentally contain letters. This check would detect the letter 'O' in place of the digit zero.

A **range check** is used to make sure that the data is inside an allowed set of values. Examination marks might have to be between 0 and 100. Checks like this are used with numeric data, but they can also be used with letters. We could check that a letter was between A and E. We can use a range of letters in the same way as a range of numbers.

Presence checks are used to make sure that a value has actually been entered in a field. We often need to make sure that vital data has not been left out when a record is created or edited.

Check digits are very useful for validating numeric data, especially if the number has many digits in it. The check digit is a single digit number calculated from all the rest of the digits in a data item, then attached to the end of the data when it is stored. Check digits are present in bar code numbers and are often used in account numbers. They can be used to detect mistakes such as reversing two digits (**transposition errors**) and a change or loss of a digit in the number. When the number is input to the computer system, the check digit is recalculated and the two versions are compared. If they match, the data is valid and can be used. If they don't match, something is wrong with the data and the number has to be re-entered. Figure 8.5 shows how the check digit is calculated for the ISBN on this book.

Parity checks are used to try to make sure data is not corrupted during transfer. Each character code is transferred together with a **parity bit**. This is a binary digit which can be either 0 or 1. Parity can be set to be either odd or even. If parity is set to be odd then the parity bit of each character is adjusted so that the total number of binary 1s transferred is odd. Figure 8.6 shows how the code for the letter 'A' is transferred using odd parity.

Even parity works in the same way but the total number of binary 1s transferred is made to be an even number. These checks will detect the change of one binary digit in the code, but if two digits are changed then the error won't be detected.

It is important to remember that, while validation checks will find data which is not sensible or reasonable and verification checks will help make sure that data is copied correctly, there is no way of making sure that the data entered into a computer system is accurate or true. The user has to make sure that the data entered is accurate, otherwise the outputs from the system will be wrong.

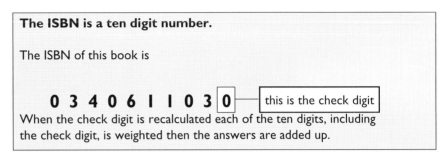

The ISBN is a ten digit number.

The ISBN of this book is

0 3 4 0 6 1 1 0 3 0 ——— this is the check digit

When the check digit is recalculated each of the ten digits, including the check digit, is weighted then the answers are added up.

ISBN	0	3	4	0	6	1	1	0	3	0	
multiply by weighting	x1	x2	x3	x4	x5	x6	x7	x8	x9	x10	
add up the answers	0	6	12	0	30	6	7	0	27	0	total is 88

Now we divide the final total by eleven. If the ISBN is valid then the remainder should equal the check digit. In this case when we divide 88 by 11 we get an exact answer with a remainder of 0. This tells us the check digit should be 0 if the ISBN is valid.

If two of the digits got mixed up we would not get a matching answer.

Figure 8.5 *Calculation of the check digit in the ISBN of* This is IS!.

The binary code used for the letter A is

| Parity bit |—| 0 | 1 0 0 0 0 0 1 |

Only seven bits are actually needed to represent the character code so bit eight is used as the parity bit.

To set odd parity we alter bit eight so that the total number of 1s in the binary number is odd. This code has two 1s so we need to set the eighth bit to 1 to make a total of three 1s.

| Parity bit |—| 1 | 1 0 0 0 0 0 1 |

Figure 8.6 *Setting odd parity on a character code.*

Saving storage space

Data files can get very big and take up a lot of space on backing store. **File compression** can be used to make the data files smaller. Compression is often used by software manufacturers to reduce the number of floppy disks needed to hold a software package. There are various methods used to compress files but one simple method is to find values which are repeated. This works well on some graphics files where the colour data for each pixel is stored. In a screen image it is common for quite large areas to be the same colour. If we have 75 red pixels it takes less space to store the number 75 and the code for the colour red than a separate value for each pixel.

Compressed files have to be uncompressed before they can be used again, so working versions aren't usually saved in compressed form, but it is useful when archive copies of data files are made. An **archive file** is one which has to be kept for a long period of time (usually for legal reasons) but which may never be used. It takes longer to get at compressed data than at uncompressed data because data has to be unpacked first. Software is also available which packs and unpacks data as it is transferred to and from disk, and makes it possible to put more data on a hard disk. Unfortunately, it does make access times much longer.

What is file compression? Why is it used and what disadvantages can it have?

What is an archive file?

CHAPTER

9

Processing Data

O nce we have stored data we nearly always have to process it in some way to produce the outputs we need.

For some applications it is sensible to process all the data at the same time as a large **batch**. This is called **batch processing**. It is suitable for applications such as producing payslips for lots of employees. Figure 9.1 shows a **system flowchart** for batch processing of payroll data.

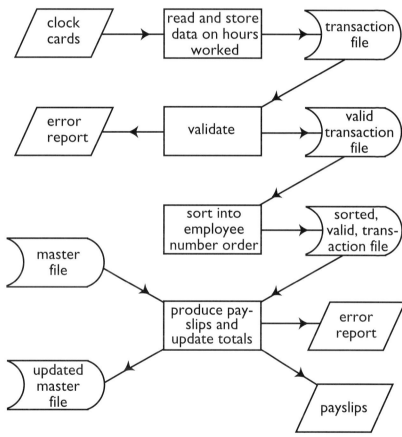

An employee using a clock card.

Figure 9.1 *System flowchart for payroll processing.*

The system flow chart shows the flow of data through the system. You can see that we have two kinds of file in this system. There is a **master file** which contains data that won't change very much, and a transaction file which contains data about the work done last month.

We will look at what happens at each stage in the process.

The first stage is to input the data and create the **transaction file**. In a large firm the data about hours worked will be collected on **clock cards** and input automatically. The photograph (above left) shows you how a clock card is used.

What does a system flow chart show?

The next stage is to validate the data in the transaction file to make sure it is sensible and can be used without problems in the later stages of processing. As a result of this stage, a valid transaction file is produced.

Now the file has to be sorted. It is sorted into the same order as the master file. If this was not done, the processing wouldn't work properly. Both files are processed **sequentially** from beginning to end and the matching records must come in the same order. A sorted, valid transaction file is produced at the end of this stage.

Batch processing can now be used to produce the payslips and update the various totals, such as pay so far this year, in the master file. In this stage a record is read from the master file and a record is read from the transaction file. The **primary key fields** are checked to make sure they match, then the pay is calculated, the payslip is printed, and fields in the master file record are altered to take account of this month's pay. The updated master file record is written to a completely new version of the master file. This stage is repeated until all the records have been processed.

Batch processing doesn't need human action once it has been started and it can't start at all until all the programs and data are ready. It is possible for errors to be found during processing and the system produces a printed **error report**. In this system it might be possible for a new employee to have a transaction file record but not have a record on the master file. This error would be reported so that the employee's pay could be worked out by hand.

Back-up files

Things can go wrong with computer systems. For example, there might be a power failure and data could be lost. It is very important to keep back-up copies of all files and to use a back-up system which makes sure that very little data will actually be lost if the system does fail.

In batch processing a back-up system called the file generation system is used. This is how it works. When processing starts the current version of the master file is referred to as the 'father' file. As a result of processing, a new version called the 'son' file is made. When processing is finished the old 'father' file is stored away, together with the transaction file. The 'father' file is now referred to as the 'grandfather' file. The 'son' file becomes the 'father' file next time processing takes place.

If anything goes wrong then the previous versions of both master and transaction files can be processed to restore the lost file. When this system is used the oldest version of the files is usually stored in a separate room or building so that if, for instance, a fire broke out in the computer department, it would be safe.

Q

What is batch processing? Suggest two applications where batch processing would probably be used.

In batch processing, the transaction file has to be sorted. What order is it sorted into and why?

Q

What is a back-up file? Why is it needed?

Describe the method of back-up used in batch processing.

Transaction processing

Some applications need to have data kept up to date all the time. These systems use **direct access files** in which any record can be read or written without having to read or write all the records before it in the file. In this sort of system records are processed immediately data is received.

A library loans system works in this way. If you borrow a book a new record is created in the loans file, and when you return a book a record in the loans file is deleted. If someone else borrows the book you have just returned then a new loans record is created. Figure 9.2 shows the system flowchart for the loans system.

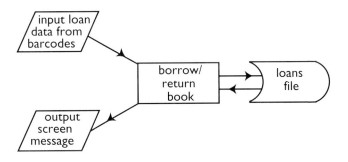

When a book is borrowed, the book number and borrower number are entered and a new loan record is created. When a book is returned, the book number is entered and the loan record is deleted.

Figure 9.2 Data flow during transaction processing.

What is transaction processing? Why might this be used in a library?

Back-up copies of the file are still needed but they are produced in a different way from back-up copies of batch processed files. Every day the loans file is copied onto magnetic tape. As each alteration is made during the day, the details of the transaction are stored on tape producing a file called the transaction log file. If the system breaks down then the transaction log file can be used to update the latest tape copy of the loans file. The only data which would be lost is the transaction being processed at the time the system failed.

Real-time processing

In this type of processing, data being inputted to the system is handled fast enough for the outputs produced to influence further inputs. **Real-time processing** is needed when computers are used to control planes, space vehicles and industrial processes. The incoming data is provided by sensors and the outputs are signals to operate engines and other control devices.

What is real-time processing? Give one example of an application where real-time processing would be needed.

What makes real-time systems very expensive?

The whole idea of real-time processing is instant response, so if the system fails, back-up copies of data files are not much use. Real-time systems are designed to make failure very unlikely. A great deal of **redundancy** is built in to the system so that if one part fails there are spares which can take over instantly, but this makes real-time systems very expensive.

10 Computer Programming Languages

Why write programs?

Sometimes we can't find an application package which can do the job we want. When this happens we have to consider writing a program using a **programming language**. All the packages, such as word processors and databases, as well as software such as operating systems, have been developed using programming languages.

There are different levels of programming language and the level that we choose depends on the task we are carrying out. A computer processor can only carry out (or **execute**) instructions in machine code, and machine code instructions consist of binary numbers. Programmers are not good at remembering the binary codes for instructions because they are all so similar. This is why programming languages were developed.

Low level languages

These languages are called **assembly languages** and they are an improvement on machine code, from the programmers point of view, because the binary instructions are replaced by short code words which are easier to remember.

In Figure 10.1 you can see a short piece of assembly language code. All that this does is swap over the contents of two locations in the computer's memory. Each instruction in this program corresponds to one machine code instruction, so getting anything useful done takes quite a lot of instructions. The programmer also needs to know a great deal about the computer hardware and how it works. In this example we have to know the addresses in memory where the data is held and something about the special memory locations, called registers, inside the CPU.

Programs written in assembly language can be very efficient when they are run because all the hardware facilities of the computer can be used exactly as required. The computer can't execute an assembly

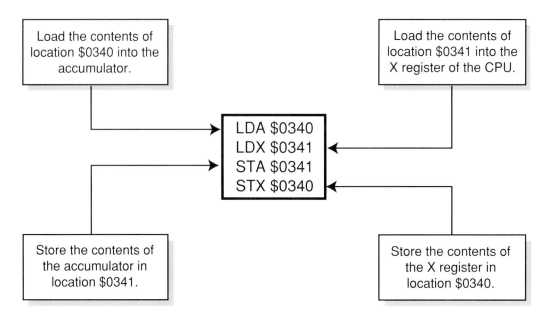

Figure 10.1 *An assembly language program.*

language program until it has been translated. A **translation program** called an **assembler** does this job. The assembler takes the assembly language program, called the **source code**, and changes each instruction into a machine code instruction. At the end of the process a new version of the program in machine code is produced. This version is called the **object code** and it can be stored so that the translation process doesn't have to be repeated every time the program is run.

High level languages

A ssembly language is a big improvement on machine code but it still isn't easy to remember the instructions. High level languages were developed to make programming easier. If you write computer programs then you will probably write them in one of the high level languages. Different languages have been developed for different purposes.

FORTRAN is a language which was developed for handling mathematical calculations in scientific and engineering applications.

COBOL was developed for writing business applications and it has good file-handling facilities.

LOGO was developed for use in education and you may be familiar with some of its graphics capabilities.

BASIC was developed as a general purpose programming language. It exists in a variety of forms, some of which are very powerful. **Visual Basic** is one of the latest versions and this is often used in developing programs which use windows, menus and control buttons because the language makes using all of these very easy.

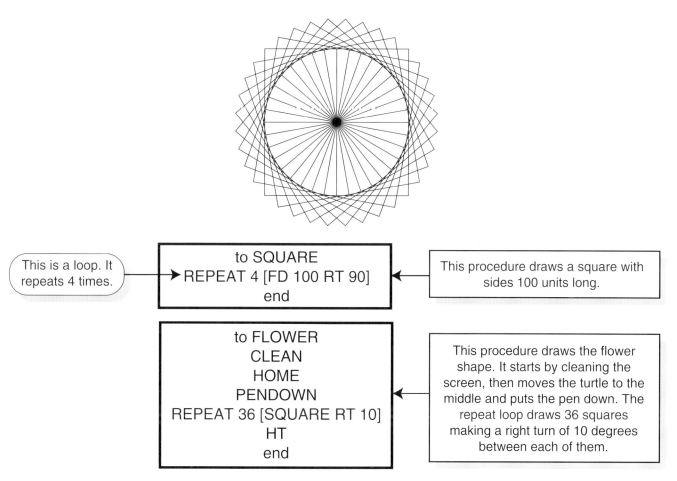

This is a loop. It repeats 4 times.

```
to SQUARE
REPEAT 4 [FD 100 RT 90]
end
```

This procedure draws a square with sides 100 units long.

```
to FLOWER
CLEAN
HOME
PENDOWN
REPEAT 36 [SQUARE RT 10]
HT
end
```

This procedure draws the flower shape. It starts by cleaning the screen, then moves the turtle to the middle and puts the pen down. The repeat loop draws 36 squares making a right turn of 10 degrees between each of them.

Figure 10.2 *A logo program to draw this flower shape.*

PASCAL is another general purpose language but, unlike many forms of BASIC, it is a **structured language** in which all variables and procedures have to be declared before they are used.

High level language programs have to be translated into machine code before they can be used but, when an instruction in a high level language is translated, it produces several machine code instructions.

The translation program used can be either an **interpreter** or a **compiler** and there are important differences between the two. An interpreter translates the high level language instructions every time the program is run. It never produces a complete object code program. This means that interpreted programs run quite slowly because of the time taken to do the translating.

They also use more memory because the translation program has to be present when the program is run. An advantage of using an interpreter is that it isn't necessary to get the whole program working to see what happens when it is run. The interpreter will execute instructions until it finds an error in the source code. Interpeters can therefore make it a little easier to develop programs.

A compiler translates all of the source code into object code and stores the object code so, once the program works properly, no more translation is needed. This means that the final program will run faster, and it will need less memory because the translation software is not needed during running.

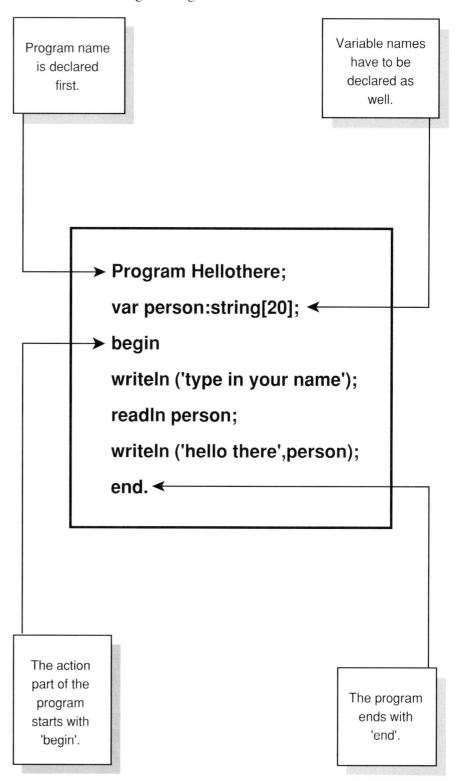

Program name is declared first.		Variable names have to be declared as well.

Program Hellothere;

var person:string[20];

begin

writeln ('type in your name');

readln person;

writeln ('hello there',person);

end.

The action part of the program starts with 'begin'.		The program ends with 'end'.

Figure 10.3 A PASCAL program

Fourth generation languages

The high level languages are a lot easier to use than assembly languages, but many of the routine tasks needed in programs still use lots of instructions. Fourth generation languages provide instructions to carry out many of these routine tasks. Database query languages are an example.

Writing programs

It is beyond the scope of this book to teach you how to write programs in a high level language, but we can give you a few guidelines. Before actually writing a program in a computer language you need to think about why you have chosen to produce a programmed solution to your problem. If you can use a package then it makes sense to do this because development will be a lot quicker.

It only makes sense to write a program if you need to get the computer to do things you can't get it to do in any other way. It is definitely not sensible to write a program for a standard database application. You would have to write all the file and record handling routines which are provided within the database package. Also, the end result would probably be less reliable and less easy to use than a database solution.

If you want to write something totally new then you will probably need to write a program. For example, if you need to produce a program combining particular examples of graphics and sounds in an interactive way, you may find you can't get the results you want in any other way.

Having decided that the effort involved in programming is worthwhile you will need to design the program very carefully and check that your design includes everything needed. You will need to break down the task into small, manageable subsections then develop a plan or algorithm to show how each of these subsections will work. More detail tends to be needed than for many package solutions to problems.

Don't start writing code until you have finished your design. It might seem as if you will get results faster if you make some parts of the program work early on, but there is no quicker way to get a program in an impossible mess than to sit down at the computer and start writing code without doing the design work first!

At some stage during the design process you will have to make a decision on the particular language you will use. Things to take into consideration are:

- How well you know the language.

- Which facilities it provides.

- Which libraries of standard routines or procedures are available.

- Whether a full version of the language is available for the computer system you use.

All computer language programs are supplied with manuals, but these are not usually the best way to learn to program in the language. There are many books available to teach you most of the popular languages. When your program is finished you should test it completely and then document it very carefully. You may have done some things in unusual ways and other programmers may find it hard to understand what you have done.

CHAPTER

11

Communications

Communications is one of the fastest growth areas of computer use. Computers can be connected to a **network**. These vary in size from links between three or four computers in a small office to the worldwide **Internet** network.

▮ *Local Area Networks (LANs)*

In a local area network the connections are made using cables. A LAN allows users to share programs and resources such as printers and backing store. It also allows users to send messages to each other using a local **electronic mail system**. This can be very convenient if people are not always in the same place as they can read their messages at any convenient network terminal.

The way in which a network is laid out is called the **network topology**. In Figure 11.1 you can see some different topologies.

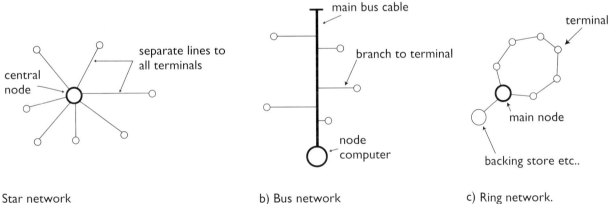

a) Star network

b) Bus network

c) Ring network.

Figure 11.1 *Star, bus and ring topologies.*

Q

What is a local area network?

What is meant by 'network topology'?

Give three advantages of using a LAN rather than having separate computers.

In a star network, all the **terminals** (computers attached to the network) are connected to one central computer called the central **node** of the network. This kind of network has some definite advantages. If one of the linking cables is damaged, only one terminal is affected and the piece of cable can be replaced quite easily. Data security is better than on other kinds of network because all data moving from one terminal to another has to go through the central node and security checking can be performed here.

In a bus network there is a long cable called the bus cable and all the terminals are attached to this. The computer responsible for all the file handling, called the file server, is also attached to this bus cable. It is not quite so easy to keep data secure on a bus network as on a star network because all data moving around the network will travel along the main bus cable as it goes to and from the file server. A fault on the main bus cable can cause problems because data won't be able to pass the faulty part of the cable.

A ring network has a loop of cable connecting all the terminals. An electronic signal called a token moves around this loop all the time. When a terminal needs to send or receive data it grabs the token so that it can use the network link. A fault on the ring cable prevents communication.

Local area networks can combine different topologies. A bus cable can have star sections connected to it. You can see a layout like this in Figure 11.2.

Q

Why is security sometimes a problem on a network?

In this network layout there is a bus cable with three star sections connected to it. At the centre of each star section is a hub which allows connection of a fixed number of terminals.

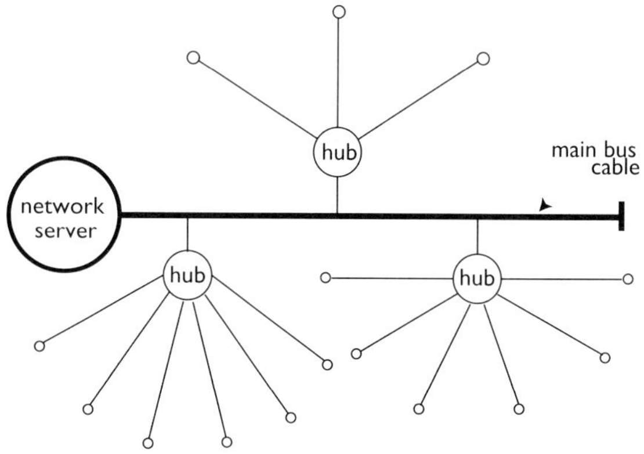

Figure 11.2 A network layout including a bus and a star configuration.

Wide Area Networks (WANs)

A **wide area network** uses telephone links to allow communication between computer systems which may be thousands of miles apart. A modem is needed to convert the data to a form which can be transmitted along telephone lines. The digital signals from the computer are used to alter a carrier signal. This is called **modulation** and happens at the modem connected to the computer system sending the data. The modem on the receiving computer extracts the digital signal by separating it from the carrier signal. This is called **demodulation**.

Data can be sent and received over a WAN in the same way as a LAN but transmission speeds are slower and, of course, use of telephone lines costs money.

Q

What is a wide area network?

Multiplexors

Multiplexors are used to combine lots of signals for transmission at one time. The separate signals are extracted after transmission by **demultiplexing**. Multiplexing is used to keep transmission costs as low as possible.

Standards and gateways

If computers in different parts of the world are going to communicate then there must be rules for transmission of data and both computers must use the same rules. There are internationally agreed standards for communication over networks but differences can still cause problems. These are overcome by using **gateways** between different networks. The gateway computer can adjust the message to meet the special requirements of each network and it can transmit data at the required speed.

Why use networks?

A local area network lets users in a business or school share resources and data. The network might allow everyone access to a high quality colour printer, for example. Sharing of data is important because lots of different people may need to use data in a shared database. The supermarket system described in chapter 18 allows all the check-out terminals to share the same product database and to update the stock details.

Local area networks can provide users with an electronic mail (e-mail) system so they can send messages to each other. An e-mail system stores messages until they are read, so if somebody is not available a message can still be left for them. The same message can be sent to lots of people at the same time. This can be useful for telling employees of a company about new developments or meetings.

Wide area networks can also provide e-mail facilities and can be used for electronic data interchange (EDI). This is transmission of data directly from one computer system to another. Examination entries can be sent from schools to examining boards in this way. The entries are prepared on the computer system and they are checked. When everything is ready, they are transmitted using communications software to make the necessary telephone connections.

The Internet is a global network. It started out as a way for businesses and universities to communicate but now has millions of users all over the world. To connect to the Internet you need a computer with a modem and an account with a service supplier

Q

What is e-mail?

What is the purpose of a modem?

which provides a gateway to the Internet. Access to the Internet is not restricted and data is available on an enormous range of subjects. You can send e-mail messages through the Internet to anyone with an e-mail address and you can also receive e-mail messages. Free software and shareware (software you try before you pay for it) is available to download onto your own system.

There is so much data available that it can be hard to find what you want, but there is searching software which helps. Even so, it is important to remember you are paying telephone charges (and probably charges to the gateway provider) for all the time you have a connection established.

The Internet has already made information available to people in all parts of the world but to get at the information the right hardware and access to a telephone system is needed. Increasingly, there is a division developing between countries which have the necessary equipment easily available and poorer countries which don't have extensive communication systems. Read the next chapter for more details on the Internet.

CHAPTER

12

The Internet

One of the most exciting and fastest growing applications of Information Technology within communications is the Internet. In 1995, it was estimated that over 350 million people had access to it and yet, for many, it appears to be something which has developed 'overnight'. It has become known as the **Information Superhighway** and has generated a great deal of new jargon.

What is the Internet?

Q

Describe the Internet in your own words.

The Internet is not just one computer, but the biggest network in the world. It is in fact a network of networks; a group of thousands of smaller computer networks, worldwide, all linked together. Some of the computers on the Internet are small PCs whilst others are large supercomputers. As the data held on any of these computers is accessible from any other on the network, the Internet, therefore, holds a vast amount of information.

The Internet, then, is not a particular place but a worldwide collection of computers all with an Internet connection. These connections may vary in size from a 2400 bps (bits per second) modem link over conventional copper telephone wires, through to massive fibre optic permanent connections which are capable of moving gigabytes of data per second. The heart of the Internet is formed from permanent lines which are capable of transferring data at rates between 64Kb/sec and 1.5Mb/sec.

The history of the Internet

The Internet began life in 1969 when the United States Department of Defence wanted a communications network which could survive in the event of a military, including nuclear, attack.

Their system was called ARPANET (Advanced Research Projects Agency Network) and it was discovered that by spreading the network out over a wide area and using a 'spider's web' of connections between computers, the system could continue to work even if sections of it were destroyed.

In 1982, ARPA established some standards governing the transfer of data between computers in order to improve the speed and reliability of this data transfer. These standards are called protocols and those developed by ARPA were called the Transmission Control

Protocol (TCP) and the Internet Protocol (IP), and we will look at these in more detail later.

In 1984, the number of hosts (computers which allow users to communicate with other computers on a network) reached 1000, and in the UK the Joint Academic Network (JANET) was set up linking major educational establishments.

In 1986, the National Science Foundation of America created five super-computing centres linked together over a network, NSFNET, which would allow researchers across America to share access to data. Since then, many different groups and organisations have joined the Internet. In 1994, there were over 3 million hosts sharing information on all sorts of topics.

How is a computer connected to the Internet?

Q

What are the two main ways of obtaining a connection to the Internet?

There are two main ways in which a user can be connected into the network. It is possible to have a permanent connection, and this may be the situation in some business organisations or universities.

Many users, however, use a **modem**, which is a device that connects the computer to a telephone line. It converts the **digital signal** produced by the computer into an **analogue signal** which can be transmitted along normal voice-carrying telephone lines.

A lap-top computer with a modem attached.

The users pay a subscription to a **service provider**, which is an organisation offering connections to the Internet. These service providers have links, or nodes, into the Internet which are often

Q

Explain the purpose of a modem in a dial-up connection to the Internet?

What is a service provider?

called **points of presence** (PoP). For many users, it is important that they choose a service provider with a PoP near to them, as their modem has to dial up a connection to it. Once connected (on-line), the user has to pay the cost of the telephone charges. A local rate call is therefore cheaper than a long distance one.

Although the Internet itself is free, it can be quite costly to tap into; a monthly subscription to a service provider plus the cost of the telephone call for every second a user is on-line. The rate at which modems can convert the signals is now very important. Whereas rates of 2400 bps were the norm in the 1980s, nowadays users should not consider a modem which is slower than 14 400 bps, and preferably choose one which can handle 28 800 bps. The faster the modem, the shorter the telephone calls to the PoP have to be.

How does the connection work?

Besides the modem and telephone link to a point of presence (or a direct connection), various pieces of software are required to be able to use the Internet.

It was mentioned above that standards, or **protocols**, had been developed in order to improve speed and reliability of data transfer over the Internet. TCP/IP system software needs to be running on the computer and its function is to make sure that any information transmitted is broken up into addressed 'chunks', or packets, and that received information is put back together in the correct order.

Q

What is TCP/IP? What job does it perform?

The way the Internet works makes this function very important. If you are sending a message to America using the Internet, you are never sure of the route it will take to get there. The first packet of information might go via France and Sweden whilst the second packet could go via a satellite link to Australia. The route does not actually matter; TCP/IP will make sure that the packets arrive in the correct place and are reassembled in the correct order, even if the second packet arrives before the first.

The protocol says that every computer on the TCP/IP network should have a unique IP 'address'. This address takes the shape of four numbers, each between 0 and 255. An example of an IP number would be 196.105.76.234 and these numbers are given out by the service providers to ensure that the same one is not used more than once. With this number, a computer on the Internet can be recognised, and it is not important where in the world it is situated. Any IP number can have a name (or **IP address**) associated with it, which can make more sense than just a set of digits.

Another piece of software is needed if the connection is made to the Internet via a modem and a service provider. This will dial up the telephone number for the point of presence and allow TCP/IP to operate on the computer.

What can the Internet be used for?

There are many ways in which the Internet can be used and, quite often, different pieces of software are required for these different uses:

ELECTRONIC MAIL

Electronic mail, or e-mail, is a way of communicating on a world-wide basis and is very fast as well as being inexpensive. To be able to use e-mail, users need an e-mail account (usually with a service provider) and are given a unique e-mail address. An example address would be: garyn@pavilion.co.uk. which you can see below.

The way e-mail works is simple. Users usually use a piece of software to prepare the message (text only) they wish to send, and tag it with the e-mail address of the person or place to which it has to be sent. This can be done off-line thus saving telephone charges. When the message(s) are ready to go, it is simply a matter of dialling up the service provider then sending the prepared mail. The transmission of data only takes a few seconds after which the telephone link can be disconnected. This means that the cost of sending the mail is cheap and costs the same whether the message is sent to someone in the same town or on the other side of the world.

Figure 12.1 E-mail software in action.

Incoming mail for a user is usually stored on a computer at their service provider and stays there until it is downloaded to the user's computer system. Again, this is done by dialling up the service provider and only takes a few seconds.

E-mail can be used for all sorts of reasons, both business and pleasure. In fact it can be used for exactly the same reasons that you would want to send a letter.

With e-mail on the Internet, it is also possible to join mailing lists. This is a way of allowing a number of people to talk about a subject using e-mail and there are hundreds of different mailing lists covering a wide variety of topics. Users join the list and, when they send a message to it, everyone else on the list receives a copy of it. Users can subscribe to mailing lists free of charge and receive regular updates on particular issues. E-mail is therefore one of the most popular and important uses of the Internet.

USENET

Whereas e-mail is a one-to-one way of sending messages, Usenet is a method of allowing thousands of people to read a particular message. It is a huge bulletin board with thousands of messages posted on it. Usenet therefore acts as a giant discussion area and, because it is so large, having so many messages on different topics, it is split up into smaller sections called **newsgroups**. These newsgroups have been categorised by topic and are subdivided within each topic. In 1995, there were over 12 000 different newsgroups covering topics from aliens to politics.

FILE TRANSFER PROTOCOL

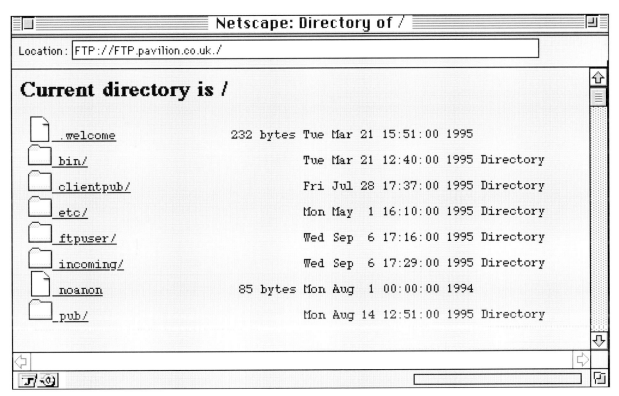

Figure 12.2 FTP software in action.

File Transfer Protocol or FTP is the method by which software and other files can be copied from one computer system on the Internet to any other. By using FTP, users can copy a program, game, image, etc. from the hard disk of another computer on the Internet onto their own. They can also send files in a similar way.

A vast number of FTP 'sites' have developed, each storing collections of programs and other files freely available to other users.

TELNET

Telnet allows users to connect their computer system to another on the Internet and act like a text-only terminal. It can be useful when users wish to run software which would not work on their own machine. Telnet is also used to log on to bulletin board systems worldwide for the cost of a local rate telephone call.

INTERNET RELAY CHAT

Internet Relay Chat or IRC is a way of using the Internet to hold a real-time conversation with another user or group of users anywhere else in the world. Like Usenet, IRC is split up into different sections called **channels**, for debate on a range of subjects. A user types in a message and other users who are taking part in the 'conversation' can see it on their display and reply to it if they want to. IRC has been described as the Internet version of CB radio.

GOPHER

One of the problems with the Internet is that there is so much information contained on the thousands of sites worldwide, that searching for a particular item can be impossible unless you know the address of the site on which it is kept. Gopher is a **menu-based system** which allows users to make choices and search for words to eventually arrive at the file they are looking for.

THE WORLD WIDE WEB

The World Wide Web (WWW or 3W) is the fastest growing part of the Internet. It is also the part which has, recently, received the most attention and hype from the media.

Its main attraction is the appearance and accessibility of its user interface. It not only allows users to read text but also allows them to see pictures and diagrams, hear music, speech and other sounds, and view movies and animation.

It started life in 1992 in Switzerland as a way of allowing scientists to exchange multimedia files. At first it too was text-based but, in 1993, the National Centre for Supercomputer Applications (NCSA) in America released a piece of software named Mosaic. This allowed graphics to be incorporated into documents and suddenly the WWW took off, growing at over 300 000% per year.

Figure 12.3 A WWW page.

The WWW is made up of millions of pages of information held on computers named Web servers. In 1995, there were over four million such pages on the Internet. These pages are connected by **hypertext links**. When a highlighted word, picture or phrase is clicked on using a pointer and mouse, a new related, or linked, page is opened on the screen. The organisation of the WWW is such that the new page can be held on a Web server on the opposite side of the world to that which held the first, but such is the beauty of the system that this does not matter to the user.

Q

Describe, in detail, three different ways in which the Internet can be used.

What is the World Wide Web? Describe how a particular page is found by a web browser.

When a link is clicked on, the software running on the user's computer, called a **web browser**, knows where to go to find the new page, as the link is actually a code which describes the address of this page. The code is called a URL or Uniform Resource Locator and an example would be: http://www.bbcnc.org.uk/index.html, which would indicate to the web browser that it needs to get a page named index.html which is on a computer named www.bbcnc.org.uk. As the page is a Web page it uses http (HyperText Transfer Protocol) to transfer it.

Web pages are written in a language called HTML or HyperText Markup Language and the web browser automatically recognises these pages and tries to display them. If the file is not an HTML page, the browser will try to start up an application to cope with it, e.g. a media player to show an animation.

It is possible to simply start at any WWW page and follow links leading to successive new pages. This idea of browsing has been given the name **surfing**, but sooner or later a user will want to search for a particular item or topic. In order to do this, search 'engines' are used. One particular engine named Lycos automatically follows links to WWW pages and adds the URL, the title of the page and the first paragraph of text to a database. This gathering of data is carried out every couple of months and, as the database is indexed, it can be searched to find particular keywords.

Anyone can create their own Web pages and these can be stored on a Web server (possibly the service provider's) for a fee and made available for anyone with access to the WWW to view. This is what makes the WWW so fascinating; that a single user can produce a page as accessible as one produced by a multinational company or a Government. Because of this, the amount of information available to users of the Internet is huge and the quality and content extremely varied.

A boy 'surfing the net' at the Cyber café.

13 Information Systems and the Law

Information systems contain important and valuable data and they allow this data to be transmitted, copied and combined in ways which were never possible with earlier manual systems. People are concerned about how **personal data** is used and who can see it, so controls on the use of this sort of data are needed.

The Data Protection Act

This law is intended to control the way in which personal data is collected and used. **Data users** who hold personal data about living people must register with the **Data Protection Registrar**. The register entry contains information about what data is stored, what it will be used for, how it is obtained and provides an address where the data user can be contacted.

As well as registering their data, the data users must make sure that they obey the **data protection principles**. These are:

1 Data must be obtained fairly and lawfully,
2 Data must be used only for the purposes stated in the register entry,
3 Data must be destroyed when it is no longer needed,
4 Data must be accurate and must be kept up to date. It must also be protected from accidental or deliberate damage,
5 Data must not be disclosed to other people who are not authorised to see it,
6 Data must be relevant for the purpose for which it is held. The amount held must not be excessive, but must be sufficient,
7 The data subject must be able to see data held about him or her, without undue delay and at a reasonable cost.

The Data Protection Act gives data subjects certain rights:

1 The data subject can see any data held about them without excessive cost or undue delay. The printout must be supplied in a readable form.
2 The data subject can demand that incorrect data is corrected or erased.
3 The data subject has a right to seek compensation for damage caused by use of inaccurate data.
4 Data subjects can also give permission for data to be disclosed.

Q

List three rights that the Data Protection Act gives to data subjects.

List four things a data user must do to comply with the Data Protection Act.

Exemptions

Some data is completely exempt from the Act. **Exemption** means that the act does not apply. Data held on paper is not subject to any regulation at all. Data held in word-processing files is exempt and so is data held for personal or recreational uses. For example, you wouldn't need to register your database of your friends' names and addresses and birthdays.

Data from which the **data subject** can't be identified is completely exempt. This category includes statistical data from surveys, provided that names are not stored. Pay-roll and pensions data is exempt, provided it is not used for anything else. Mailing lists are also exempt provided that the data does not include anything except name and address.

As well as these full exemptions there are also quite a lot of **partial exemptions**. These allow some of the principles to be ignored.

Data can be exempt from the rule about unauthorised disclosure. This exemption is granted if data is needed to help prevent crime. It is also granted if data is needed for tax purposes or if the law requires data to be made public. Disclosure exemption can be allowed in the interests of national security but this requires a special certificate from a government minister.

Access exemption removes the data subject's right to see what is stored about them. Data which has to be kept secret for the prevention of crime and catching of criminals can be given this exemption. Data used to make decisions on appointment of judges and other people in the judicial system is also not revealed to the data subjects. Health and social services data can also be given this exemption if it is considered not to be in the data subject's best interest for them to see what is held.

Access exemptions can be allowed in the interests of national security. This also needs a certificate signed by a government minister.

Q

List three kinds of data which are completely exempt from the Data Protection Act.

How does the Data Protection Act work?

The ideas behind the Act are good but it doesn't always work as well as it should. We all receive lots of junk mail and this use of data is perfectly legal. If you order something by post or phone you often give permission for personal data to be disclosed without intending to do this. Most mail order firms expect you to say if you don't want personal data to be passed on to other firms. You have to put a cross in a box and it isn't always in an obvious place on the form.

Many people think that data subjects must be informed when data is stored about them, but this isn't true. Data subjects have to work out who might hold data and then ask to see the data. There is also the question of cost: what is a reasonable charge for a printout from one database may not seem so reasonable if data is held in ten separate databases and a charge is made for each one.

The relevance of data is sometimes questioned. What the **data user** and data subject think is relevant can be very different. If a bank stores data about the political views of its customers, is this relevant to the purpose of handling the customers' accounts?

There are ways around the law. Data kept in computer files can be just references to data on paper which isn't covered at all. Many data users don't bother to register anyway, either because they don't know that they should, because they think their data is exempt, or because they don't think it matters.

Copyright law

The **copyright law** makes it illegal to produce extra copies of software for sale or to use on extra machines. Software theft, sometimes called **software piracy**, is a real problem for the industry. Developing new software packages is expensive and if people steal software instead of buying it the developers don't get the income they expect.

The **Federation Against Software Theft** works hard to catch people and firms who use illegal copies of software. A typical problem is the company which buys a software package and has a license to use it on a limited number of network terminals. It then gets used on many more terminals than it should, but nobody buys the extra licence. Networks can have software installed which counts the number of users of each package and refuses to load packages onto more than the allowed number of terminals at one time. Large firms are beginning to take their responsibilities more seriously and are setting up controls to prevent employees bringing in unauthorised software to use at work, or making copies of software to use at home.

Large scale duplication of software for resale also happens. A person who makes and sells these copies is breaking the law. Sometimes the software is bought as a genuine version of the package. The user only finds out it is a copy when they ring the manufacturer for support.

Q

What is meant by software piracy?

The Computer Misuse Act

This Act was introduced to try to control 'hacking'. A **hacker** is someone who makes unauthorised access to computer systems and data belonging to someone else. They may steal the data or they may deliberately alter it in some way, perhaps by introducing a computer virus into the system.

Hackers quite often break into the system just to prove they can beat the system security. The damage to data sometimes caused accidentally can be expensive to repair, but when the data is deliberately altered the effects can be worse. Small alterations may not be noticed for some time but often have serious consequences.

Hackers are a serious problem, but a much bigger problem can be someone working with the system or in the building who wants to deliberately damage the data. This person may have the right to use the system anyway or may find it very easy to get through the security system. **Passwords** help to keep systems secure but they only provide good security if they are changed often, are not obvious and are kept secret by those who need to know them. Read Chapter 14 for more on data security issues.

Q

What is meant by the term 'hacker'? Why can hacking cause problems to owners of computer systems?

CHAPTER

14

Data Security

Why must data be kept secure?

Data has value to the people who own it and use it in their business. If data is lost, damaged or stolen it can have a disastrous effect on a business. It is very important that data is kept as safe as possible and that, if something does go wrong, little or no data is lost.

Keeping data safe

Data can be lost or damaged by accident and most data loss is the result of an accident or carelessness. It can also be erased or altered deliberately and this kind of damage must be guarded against as well.

Accidental damage can happen if disks and tapes are handled or stored carelessly. Magnetic fields can damage data on magnetic disk or tape. Electric motors, monitors, power cables and telephones can all produce magnetic fields so we need to be careful about where disks and tapes are stored. You can see how tapes are often stored in the photograph (below).

Tapes and disks must be stored safely.

Floppy disks and tapes can melt even if they don't burn.

Excessive heat and moisture can also damage disks and tapes. They should always be kept in dry places where they won't get too hot. **Back-up copies** need to be stored in containers which are fire- proof and heat-proof. Metal containers can become heated up in a fire and the tapes and floppy disks will then melt and be useless, like the ones in the photograph (left).

Dirt on disks and tapes can also lead to data loss. Dirt can come from many sources such as dust, fingers, crumbs, hair or smoke.

A dirty working environment can cause damage to storage media and data.

The whole of a disk or tape can be affected and, as well as damaging the data, the dirty tape or disk can damage the drive in which it is placed. The best way of preventing this kind of data loss is to make sure that the working environment is clean.

Sometimes data is lost because the person using the computer system is not sure what to do next. Software can be designed so that any situation that might result in data loss produces a **warning message**. The user has to **confirm** the action before it takes place by pressing a key or clicking on a button on the screen. This sort of warning will be produced if the user attempts to delete all the records in a file, or to write new data over an existing file. It is impossible to protect all data in this way because questioning every operation would make software unusable. A balance must be found between keeping the data safe and producing a system that works quickly.

Computer viruses can cause data corruption and data loss. The chances of a virus getting onto a computer system can be reduced if certain rules are always obeyed. Many businesses have a set of rules and anyone breaking them is likely to be dismissed. These rules usually forbid the use of floppy disks which have been written outside the building without a virus check being run first. The use of unauthorised software is also forbidden because viruses often get onto office machines when employees decide to install extra

Q

Give three ways in which data can be damaged accidentally.

What precautions can be taken to prevent accidental damage to data?

Why is it important to run virus checking software all the time?

How can software help to prevent accidental data loss?

software. Access to other systems through a modem can also be restricted. It is essential to run **virus checks** at frequent intervals or to have virus-detecting software active all the time, because viruses often don't activate themselves straight away.

Deliberate attacks on software are more difficult to guard against, especially if a computer system is part of a wide area network using phone lines for communication. Data can be deleted, altered or simply stolen and it is vital to prevent unauthorised people getting access to the data. The precautions taken depend on the value and sensitivity of the data which is stored.

It is important that computer terminals are switched off when left unattended for a long period of time. A terminal like the one (below) that is not only turned on, but left with a screenful of sensitive data displayed to anyone passing by, is obviously an easy target.

A passer-by could read this data and possibly make alterations.

This lock prevents unauthorised entry to the computer area.

Computer systems that store sensitive or valuable data may need to be kept in buildings with restricted access. Magnetic strip cards can be used to operate door locks to get into the room. Other kinds of lock need code numbers entered on a keypad before the door will open.

A system of **passwords** can be used so that access to the data is restricted. The password system is **hierarchical**, with different passwords giving different levels of access to the data. At the lowest level, the password will allow the user **read-only access** to some of the data in the system. This means that staff with this password can see a limited amount of data but can't change anything. Higher level passwords will give both **read and write access** to the data, although not necessarily to all of the data in the system. The top password will allow read and write access to all data files, but very few people will know this code.

How can unauthorised access to data be prevented?

Give an example of a good password. Explain why this password is likely to be effective.

When setting up password systems it is best to use **numeric or alphanumeric codes** and these should be reasonably long. It takes far longer to try all possible combinations of letters and numbers of a six character code than for a three character code. Real words should be avoided because people often choose words that mean something special to them and these can be easily guessed. Passwords and codes should never be written down and left near the computer.

To make sure a password system stays effective it is vital that passwords are changed frequently. The exact timing of changes will depend on how important the data is, but it is never a good idea to make password changes on the same day every week. If it is generally known that the passwords change on a Friday night, then anyone planning to break into the system will just make sure they do it before the change.

The system itself can keep a check on all attempts to log on. It will store details of all passwords used, the times at which users logged on and off, and a list of all files accessed with the level of access allowed. It will also store the exact times at which changes were made to the files. This kind of **log file** can be useful if unauthorised access is suspected, because the list produced can often track down the terminal and password used. The system logs all attempts to get at data, whether or not they are successful, so it can provide a warning that someone is trying to break in. If attempts to enter the system are being made using a **modem**, the system can store the phone number from which the call was made. All this makes it easier to catch people trying to damage or steal data.

What happens when something goes wrong?

Sometimes, although every possible precaution has been taken, data is lost or damaged. What happens to remedy the problem depends on just how badly the data is damaged. Most of the time, provided that back-up copies are available, the data can all be restored very quickly and business can continue as normal.

If the damage has been caused by a virus then virus-killing software will be used to remove it from fixed backing store such as hard disks. Damaged data is then restored from clean back-up copies if necessary. Tapes and floppy disks which may contain the virus can be checked and the virus removed, but it is often more cost effective simply to replace all the suspect disks and tapes.

All data-users should have some kind of **disaster recovery plan** so that very serious losses of data and hardware do not lead to the business closing down. A plan for this may involve a contract for supply of replacement computer hardware at short notice, or may be an arrangement for the use of an alternative site if a building is

What is a disaster recovery plan?

damaged too badly to be used. When making this kind of plan it is important to be sure that recent data is stored away from the main building, otherwise all the replacement equipment will be useless. How far away the data should be kept depends on the nature of the threat. In an earthquake area it isn't much use keeping the back-up copies of data a few hundred metres away. Data can easily be transmitted to remote sites, so often data is store in offices many miles away.

Data theft

When data is stolen it can represent a huge problem for a business. Data theft can occur when the actual storage medium is stolen in a burglary. The thief who takes a personal computer takes all the data on the hard disk at the same time. In this case, problems can arise if the data is particularly sensitive. All sensitive data should be **encrypted** so that it makes no sense when it is read back without using the appropriate de-encryption software. It should also be protected by a good password system. These measures are usually enough to prevent a casual thief from reading the stolen data.

Data can also be stolen by making copies of the data files. The user may not be aware that the theft has taken place until customers start to buy the products or services elsewhere. Again, encryption of data can make it useless to a thief. A good security system, which records all attempts to access data, will help to find out how and when the theft took place and may provide information on who the thief was.

It is also important to remember that lots of data ends up as information on print-outs which may be discarded at the end of the day. The easiest way to steal information is often to get it out of the dustbin! All print-outs containing valuable information should be shredded before being discarded.

What are the main threats?

Accidental damage is the main cause of data loss. This is most often a result of carelessness by employees.

Deliberate damage is most often caused by employees of a business, and the worst damage can be caused by staff who work with the system and have high level access rights to the data. This is why, when staff who work at this level have to be dismissed, they are not allowed to go near the computer system.

Data theft can happen as a result of **hacking** into a system, but data is most often stolen by employees or in situations where a large system is shared by several companies.

15 Developing Information Systems

If an information system is going to be satisfactory it is important to be very clear about what the system must do. This may seem obvious, but many systems have been unsuccessful because nobody has managed to work out what is really needed. The process of finding out about the system requirements is called **analysis**.

Analysis

In many ways this is the most important stage in system development. Mistakes made in the analysis stage are difficult to correct later. Usually a computer system is developed to replace an existing manual system, or a simpler computer system, so a good starting point for analysis is to look at the existing system. We need to find out how the system works, what improvements are needed and what future developments may need to be considered.

We can find out about an existing system in several different ways. We can observe the system being used as this will let us see what happens to data entering the system and what outputs are produced. Effective observation takes time; you won't find out very much by watching for just half an hour. Observation is useful because we can often see things happen which might not be described by any of the people working with the system. We can also see the conditions under which the system is used and this can be important.

An interview session.

List four ways of finding out about data flow in existing systems.

Poor analysis leads to information systems which don't meet user requirements. Why?

Talking to people who work with the existing system may also help. People working at different levels may have different views about what is good or bad about this system. An interview like the one in the photograph (opposite) can be a good way to find out what they think.

Questionnaires can be used if there are lots of people involved. A questionnaire can be useful anyway because people can take time to think and they are often more willing to write down what they think about an existing system than to say it in front of others. Always remember that people can feel threatened by the idea of introducing a computer system. A tactful approach works best.

It is a good idea to describe the existing system, including the way data flows through it, so we can be sure we know how it works. Diagrams can be drawn to help make things clear.

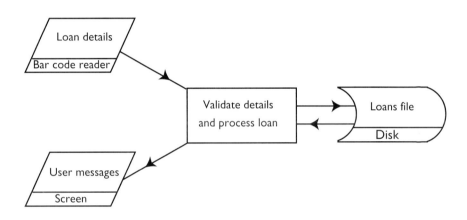

Figure 15.1 System flow chart for a library system.

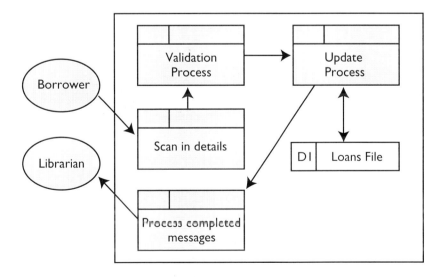

Figure 15.2 Dataflow diagram for a library system.

At this stage we may need to produce a **feasibility report** before doing any more work. In this we will explain whether a new computer system would be better than the existing system, giving reasons for our recommendations. This report should show, in outline, what could be achieved with the new system.

Assuming that the feasibility report shows that the new system is a good idea, we carry out furthur analysis to allow us to make a list of everything the new system has to be able to do. The list will include all of the outputs which have to be produced and all of the special user requirements as well. This is called the **requirement specification**.

A requirement specification needs to be reasonably detailed as it forms the basis for the later stages in producing the system. It must be written in a way that the people using the system will be able to understand and must be checked with the users to make sure that the system will do everything required. It also has to be checked to make sure that the list of requirements is consistent. For example, a user may want a system to be developed using a particular database package and also want it to store pictures. If the package won't allow pictures to be stored then these requirements conflict. All conflicts have to be sorted out before anything else is done. In this case the user would have to decide whether to use a different package or do without the pictures.

Users are sometimes rather unrealistic about what can be achieved with existing hardware and software. The requirement specification must not include anything which cannot possibly be provided.

The requirements specification can be used to check the system is being built properly and as the basis for evaluation of the completed system.

Q

What is a feasibility study?

What makes a particular problem suitable for computerisation?

What is a requirements specification? What is it used for?

▮ *Design*

We now move on to design the system which meets the agreed specification. There may be several possible approaches to producing a working system and we should consider all of them carefully before deciding which one to use.

Large systems can be broken down into subsystems which are easier to work with. We need to look at what the system has to do and divide up these functions into sensible groups. A library system has to provide information about books, members and loans. As well as providing all the outputs needed, we have to be able to add, edit and delete data about these three things. We can divide this system into three main areas:

- the catalogue section,
- the members section,
- the loans section.

Each of these sections can be divided up into smaller tasks relating to data input, data processing and data output.

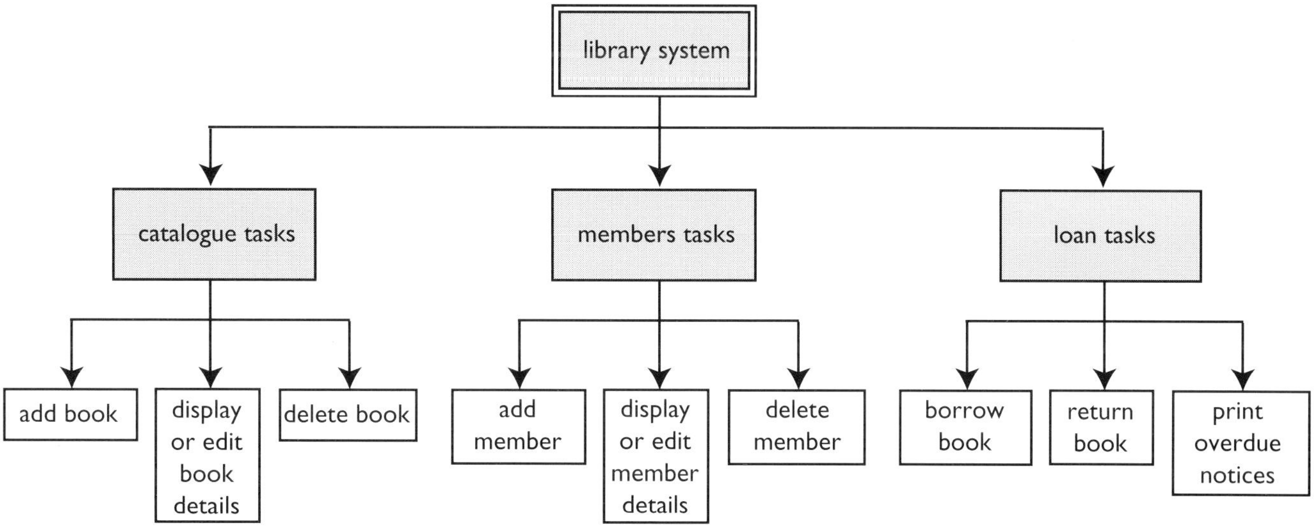

Figure 15.3 *Tasks in a library system.*

The structure diagram in Figure 15.3 is one way of showing how the parts of the system are connected. The way in which the system interacts with the user needs a lot of consideration. This **Human Computer Interface** needs to be consistent throughout the system. Some points to consider are as follows.

USE OF COLOUR

Colour can be useful to highlight messages but too many different colours can be confusing. Care needs to be taken to make sure colours give good contrast so words are readable. Red is a warning colour so it is probably best to reserve it for warning messages. Remember - some people are colour blind and have problems distinguishing certain colours so it is best to avoid combining red and green or blue and yellow.

SOUND

Sound should be reserved for situations where it is essential. Music systems need sound but it would be a distraction in a spreadsheet system. Warning sounds can be used, but don't overdo it! If the sounds come too often and without a good reason the user will get annoyed and will probably turn the sound off altogether.

FLASHING SYMBOLS

These can attract user attention, but be very careful. Certain flash rates can cause some people to have epileptic fits.

LOCATION OF ITEMS ON THE SCREEN

Try to keep the same items in the same place on all the screens. Users tend to look mostly at the top third of the screen and are less likely to see the bottom corners. Error messages are not likely to be seen if they are tucked away at the bottom of the screen.

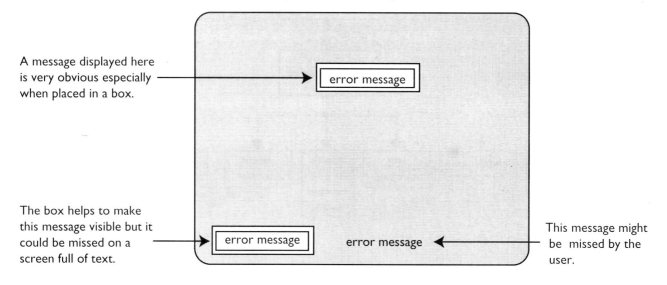

A message displayed here is very obvious especially when placed in a box.

error message

The box helps to make this message visible but it could be missed on a screen full of text.

error message

error message

This message might be missed by the user.

Positioning of error messages on the screen needs care. Don't put them in corners or right at the bottom.

Figure 15.4 *Positioning of error messages on the screen.*

MOVING FROM SCREEN TO SCREEN

Always use the same method to move between screens and remember to tell the user how to do this. It is irritating if some screens need just a key-press, but others need a specific word followed by pressing the 'enter' key.

MAKING CHOICES

If the user has to make choices, decide whether to use the mouse or the keyboard, or allow use of either. Don't use the mouse for some choices and the keyboard for others. This makes it much harder for the user to learn to use the system.

APPROPRIATE USE OF LANGUAGE

Make sure the words you use are suitable for the eventual user of the system. Avoid too much use of technical terms. Don't use long words if your system is for young children. In some cases pictures work better than words.

When designing a human computer interface there are many things to be considered. Describe two and say why you think they are important.

Detailed design

Working from the outputs needed for each task we can decide what information will be needed to make the system work. We have to work out how this information will be collected and how it will be converted to data to be stored in the system.

In the case of the library system we need to work out the record structures we require, making sure all the data needed is included. A system flowchart can show us how data will move through the library system.

For each section we have identified we need to produce detailed designs. We will need plans for screen layouts and for printed outputs. These designs can be drawn on squared paper, to make sure everything will fit.

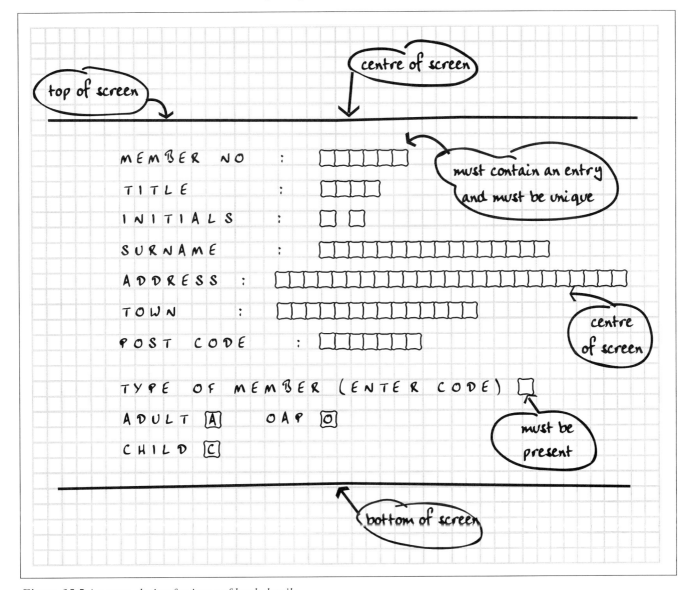

Figure 15.5 A screen design for input of book details.

We also need to design the processing the system will have to do. This may be searching, sorting, performing calculations or producing graphics. The amount of design work needed here will depend on how we plan to solve the problem. If the solution is based on an existing package, such as a spreadsheet or database package, we can produce simple descriptions of what we need to do because the package will do most of the work. This description of what must be done is called an **algorithm**.

Sometimes there isn't a suitable package and we need to write a program of our own. In this case we need to produce a more detailed algorithm to explain how the program will work.

There are various ways of describing algorithms including structure diagrams, pseudocode and flowcharts. A structure diagram for a program is quite like the one for the library system tasks in Figure 15.3 but it shows more detail and indicates where decisions will be made and where choices are available. If an action is repeated then this is also shown on the structure diagram.

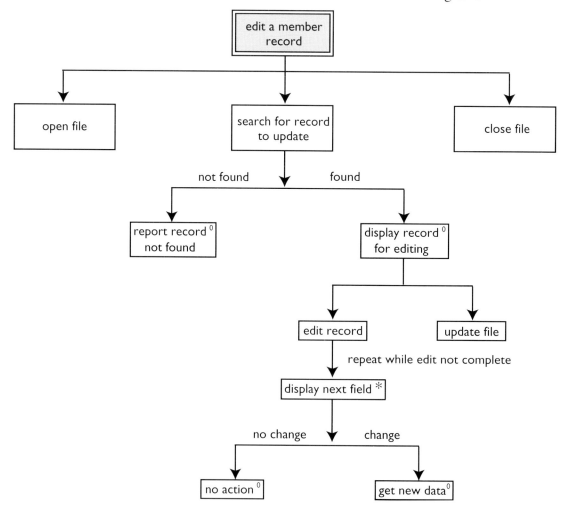

Figure 15.6 *Structure diagram for editing a member record in the library system.*

The final design needs to contain enough detail to allow any competent person to carry out implementation.

As well as designing the actual system we need to design **test data** which will let us check that the whole system works as it should. The general principle of testing is to check that the system works properly with typical data, data at the limits of what is allowed and data which is wrong. We also need to check that the system meets all of the requirements in the specification and will be acceptable to the user. Designing the tests at this stage makes it more likely that we will test what the system should do rather than simply show what it can do.

Q

What kind of data should be used to test a computer system?

Implementation

During implementation we use whatever software and hardware we have selected to set up the system and get it to produce the required outputs. Each section identified in the design should be tackled in turn. It is sensible to start with the most essential parts of the system and not the parts which don't really matter very much. In the library database system the parts which handle the data files are more important than producing a pretty introduction screen.

Testing can be carried out as each section is completed, but it is important to test the whole system when it is finished. Sometimes problems occur when the parts are put together and, if we don't carry out a full **system test**, we won't find these problems.

Documentation

The final stage is writing the **documentation** needed for the users of the system. This is often divided into sections. There is one section for people who have to maintain the system and therefore need to know a lot of detail about how it works. A different kind of documentation is needed for the people who will use the system every day. In our example, the librarian doesn't need to know how the system works but does need to know how to carry out the tasks the system can do.

Maintenance documentation contains details of how the system was designed and set up. It also contains test data and results of testing. It needs a contents page and an index to make it easy to use.

The user guide needs to be carefully organised so that the various jobs the system can do are described in a sensible order. Illustrations can be used to make instructions clearer. It is important to describe things that might go wrong as well, and explain how to put these things right. Don't forget that back-up copies are sometimes needed when things go wrong. You need to explain how to make these and how to use them. The user guide also needs a contents page and an index.

Q

Name three topics which should be included in a user guide for an information system.

CHAPTER

16

Banking

B anks are a common feature in many High Streets but the functions that they carry out are often taken for granted.

There are many different ways in which money can change hands between one person or organisation and another. Cash can be used, but credit cards, cheques, direct debit and standing orders are popular ways of paying or receiving money. In banking, the majority of transactions involve no cash whatsoever, but simply the addition or subtraction of sums of money from computers.

Cheques

B anks in the UK all use the same system for processing cheques. A cheque, like the example in Figure 16.1, is like a letter instructing the bank to transfer an amount of money from one person's or organisation's bank account to another.

Figure 16.1 A cheque.

When a person opens a current bank account they are issued with a book of cheques which can be used only by them. Some building societies also have cheque books as part of their current account facilities. Each cheque is pre-printed with many details such as the serial number of the cheque, the code for the bank and branch where this person holds the account, and the customer's account number, as in Figure 16.2.

    ‖ 205517 ‖   3 1 ⠐⠂22 04   12 34 5678 ‖

Figure 16.2 The three pre-printed codes along the bottom of the cheque.

These three sets of numbers are printed along the bottom of the cheque using magnetic ink and in a particular style which you can see in Figure 16.3. These numbers can be automatically read by a machine using a process called **Magnetic Ink Character Recognition (MICR)** (see Chapter 3).

Figure 16.3 *The MICR character set.*

Although printing cheques with magnetic ink is more expensive than with ordinary ink, it means that they can always be read automatically. This will be possible even if the characters in the codes have been tampered with, either deliberately or by accident. For example, the cheque may get dirty. Other details printed on the cheque use ordinary ink. These usually include the customer's name, the bank's name and address and the sort code, as these do not need to be read automatically.

Some details cannot be pre-printed on the cheques, for instance the amount to be paid (both in words and in numbers), the person or organisation to which the money is to be paid, the date the cheque was filled in and the customer's signature. Space is left on the cheque for the customer to fill in these details.

So how does the money get from one bank account to another once the cheque has been written, especially as the people involved may have accounts with different branches of the same bank or with different banks in different towns? The transaction process happens in the following way.

Q

Explain in your own words how MICR is used in banking.

1 A cheque is given from one person or organisation to another.

2 The person or organisation who receives the cheque presents it at the bank.

3 The bank prints the amount of money using MICR on the right hand side of the bottom line on the cheque.

4 If the cheque comes from an account belonging to the same branch as the one at which it was presented for payment, the cheque's details are entered into the branch computer where the amounts in both bank accounts involved are adjusted accordingly.

5 If the cheque comes from an account in a different bank or another branch of the same bank then a process called **clearing** takes place. This happens as follows:

   a) Cheques go to the bank's main clearing house, used by all its branches.

   b) Cheques are swapped with those from other banks so that each bank receives all its own cheques.

c) The bank's main computer reads all the cheques and sorts them out into branches.

d) The cheques are sent back to branches where the accounts are held in order to check details such as dates and signatures.

e) Any payments which the branch decides should not go ahead are transmitted to the bank's main computer.

f) All other payments go ahead, i.e. they are 'cleared'.

The whole process usually takes three to five days.

Automated Teller Machines (ATMs)

Over recent years, it has been much easier to obtain cash and some other services from your bank account. This is due to the number of **Automated Teller Machines (ATMs)** which have been installed. These can be found not only outside banks but at supermarkets, service areas on motorways and many other locations.

These ATMs, often referred to as 'hole in the wall' machines or cashpoints, are linked to the bank's main computer. In order to use the ATM, the customer requires a card issued by the bank. On the back of this plastic card is a magnetic strip which holds the customer's account number. You can see one of these in Figure 16.4.

Figure 16.4 The front and back of a credit/debit card.

When the card is inserted into the machine, the account number is read from the magnetic strip on the back of the card and is used to access the customer's record on a file in the bank's main computer. This record contains many details including the **Personal Identification Number (PIN)** belonging to the customer, and the amount of money in the account, called the account balance.

The customer is asked, usually via a small monitor built into the machine, to enter their PIN. This PIN is known only to the customer and the bank and is used to make sure the card is being used by the correct person. The number is typed in using the keypad on the ATM, but does not show up on the monitor for security reasons.

Q

Explain the meaning of the following abbreviations:

MICR

ATM

PIN

An automated teller machine.

If the PIN entered does not match up with the one held by the bank's computer, a message is displayed asking for the number to be re-entered. If three incorrect attempts are made to enter a PIN then the person using the card is prevented from obtaining any cash and the card is kept inside the machine to be collected by an employee of the bank at some time during the day. Damaged cards are also retrieved by the bank in this way.

If the PIN does match up, the customer is offered a number of services, again via the monitor. These include the withdrawal of cash, ordering of statements, requests for new cheque books and obtaining the balance of the account.

If a cash withdrawal is required, the customer enters the amount they wish to obtain. This is checked against the balance of the account and, if sufficient funds are available, the machine dispenses the bank notes. At the same time, the amount withdrawn is subtracted from the balance on the customer's record on the main computer. When the transaction is finished, the card is finally released back to the customer by the machine.

ATMs have revolutionised the way in which people obtain cash. In the past, bank customers who wanted to withdraw cash had to go to a bank during its opening hours, usually 9.00 am to 3.30 pm, Monday to Friday. Now cash can be obtained 24 hours a day, seven days a week from a variety of locations.

Today, many banks share ATM facilities, with any particular ATM allowing access to accounts from a number of different banks. Many banks now have ATMs inside the bank, allowing customers to withdraw cash and perform other services without having to be served by a bank clerk who may also be dealing with customers' deposits and other enquiries.

In the future, the nature of banking may alter even further. Debit cards such as Switch and Delta allow funds to be taken immediately from one bank account and transferred to another without the use of

Q

Describe the component parts of an ATM.

Describe the process by which a customer obtains cash from an ATM.

Explain the ways in which ATMs have revolutionised the way people obtain cash.

A Mondex reader.

cheques. This **Electronic Funds Transfer** does away with the clearing process and the time delay imposed by this form of processing.

Home banking facilities are now on offer from some banks and allow customers to carry out financial activities such as ordering statements, obtaining a balance, paying bills, etc. using either the telephone or a home computer equipped with a modem.

Cash is still used for many transactions, particularly small purchases. One recent development, however, is promising to move us nearer to becoming a 'cashless society'. The NatWest and Midland banks have developed a special bank card called a Mondex card, which is very different from the credit or debit cards which have been mentioned earlier.

The Mondex card is a smart card (see Chapter 3) which contains a microchip that can hold electronic cash. The card comes with a Balance Reader which displays how much money is stored on the card at any given time. You can see one in the photograph (left).

Any amount of cash, large or small, from the cardholder's bank account can be transferred and stored on this card. Electronic money from the card can also be transferred into a bank account. This transfer from bank account to card and vice versa can happen in a number of different ways:

1 A person's card can be inserted into specially adapted ATMs which recharge the card with electronic money, taking the equivalent amount out of their bank account. Money can also be taken off the card and added to the person's bank account. This ATM can also tell the person the amount remaining on the card, and give a statement of the last ten transactions carried out using the card.

2 A special Mondex telephone with a smart card reader can be used. This will be available for home and business use and can transfer the cash to and from a bank account 24 hours a day, every day of the year for the price of a local telephone call. This telephone, which also works as a normal telephone, has a built-in screen on which can be displayed the balance of a card or its linked bank account, and a list of the last ten transactions. It can also transfer electronic cash to and from any other Mondex card inserted into another Mondex telephone, lock or unlock a card and set or change the Personal Code of any card (see later).

3 Special public payphones will be available which work in the same way as the Mondex telephone and offer the same functions.

4 Mondex-compatible mobile phones will be able to act as personal mobile cash dispensers.

Once the card is charged with an amount of electronic money and unlocked by using a Personal Code, it can be used in the same way as cash. Once unlocked, the card stays that way until locked again using the Personal Code.

Retailers (those who sell any goods or services) can have a special, mains-powered terminal like the one in the photograph (below). Small traders, like newspaper-sellers, can use battery powered terminals. Payments for any goods or services purchased are made by inserting the customer's card into a card reader in this retail terminal. Funds are transferred immediately from the card to the terminal with no need for signatures or authorisation. Inside the retail terminal is one of the retailer's Mondex cards and the cash is transferred onto this. The retailer can deposit these takings at any time, e.g. at the end of the day, using the special ATMs, telephones or payphones.

A Mondex retail terminal.

A Mondex wallet.

Unlike credit cards, which are unlikely to be used to buy something costing just a few pence, the Mondex card can be used for any purchase. Retailers should find that there are many benefits in using this type of card. They receive cash instantly as there is no waiting for a cheque to clear, so payment is faster. There is no need to fill out a cheque and verify a bank card, and very small purchases as well as very large ones can take place. The only limit is the amount of money the customer has remaining on his or her card.

The purchase of goods and services, however, is only one way in which cash is used by society. Money changes hands between individuals, other than retailers, for a variety of purposes. For this reason, a special Mondex 'wallet' is available, which you can see (left). This wallet allows people to keep a separate store of electronic money, for example at home, and only carry a minimum amount on their card. This gives cardholders some security as, if they lose their card, only that minimum amount is lost with it.

Transfers between individuals can also be made by inserting the card into the electronic wallet and moving cash from the first person's card to the recipient's card. For example, parents could transfer an amount to a child's card as pocket money. The wallet could also be used by a retailer, such as a taxi driver who is constantly on the move, as a simple retail terminal.

In everyday use, these electronic transactions are anonymous, just like cash. If a card is lost, a unique identity number stored on the chip, which will have been registered alongside the customer's personal details at their bank, may be used in order to return the card to its owner.

As mentioned previously, a cardholder can use their Personal Code to lock their card and prevent unauthorised access. A card has to be in its unlocked state for any transfers to take place.

Each time the card is used the chip generates a unique digital code which can be recognised by the other Mondex card in the transaction. This unique code is the guarantee that the cards involved are genuine Mondex cards and that the transaction data has not been tampered with.

Although the Mondex card is relatively new in this country, it is seen as being usable worldwide. It uses a set of symbols which are independent of any language so that users can complete transactions anywhere in the world where they see the Mondex sign. Five different currencies can be held at any one time on separate 'pockets' in the card's microchip so travellers can use their cards abroad.

This type of card will be useful in conjunction with many of the new applications of Information Technology which are about to become commonplace. For example, anyone will be able to use these cards to pay for Video on Demand movies and games supplied by cable into the home. This will avoid building up debts on the phone bill or bank account, as it is only possible to spend what is on the card.

It will be interesting to see how far this development and others lead us along the path to a truly cashless society.

Examine the prospect of systems like Mondex producing a 'cashless' society.

17 A Mail-Order and Wholesale Business

Information systems are very important in the increasingly competitive mail-order business. The business we will look at sells computer systems and a wide range of computer components. Some of its trade is mail-order but most of the customers buy large quantities direct for use in their own businesses.

A warehouse containing computer components and systems ready for dispatch to customers.

As well as basic stock level information, this company needs to keep track of individual customer accounts, returned goods, and payment for **cash-on-delivery** items. There is a network of personal computers with terminals in the accounts department, sales department, technical department and the warehouse. There are separate stock, order, returns and accounts files, but these are all tables within a relational database so there are links between the files. The links are shown in Figure 17.1. Remember, we can only have a link between files (tables) if they have a common field. There shouldn't be more than one common field to link two tables. You can see that customer number, order number and stock number are important linking fields.

Q

Why is a network needed for this application?

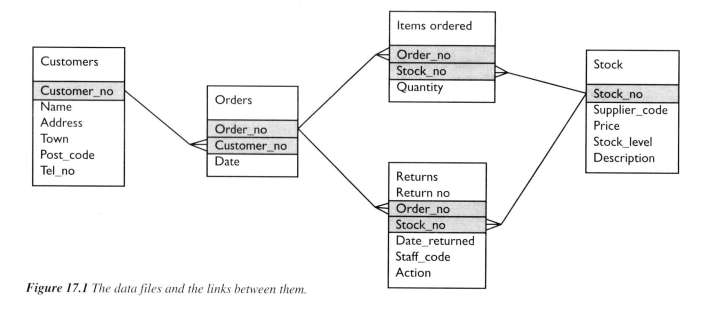

Figure 17.1 *The data files and the links between them.*

Q

How does the system prevent people returning things they bought somewhere else?

Why do items have to be tested when they are returned?

A technician tests a faulty item to make sure it really doesn't work.

Q

What is the purpose of the returned items report?

The returns system

The part of the system we will look at in detail deals with the returns. If an item purchased by a customer doesn't work as it should, it is sent back. A business like this with a very large turnover will inevitably have some items returned as faulty. All returned items have to be booked into the system. To make sure people don't return components bought elsewhere, or return them a long time after they were bought, the returns system looks up the record in the order file using the order number to find out when the order was placed.

If the item can be accepted, a record is created in the returns file. At this stage, the faulty item is tested by one of a team of technicians. Sometimes items are returned when there is really nothing wrong with them because the buyer didn't know how to connect the part properly. Items that work are not replaced so every item is tested by a technician, as can be seen in the photograph (left). When the technician tests an item he or she enters the result of the test and his or her identification number into the item record. If the item works, it is returned to the customer and the record in the return file is altered to show that this has happened.

Items which test as faulty are returned to the original supplier and the customer gets a new one as a replacement. It is very important that the system keeps a check on how many items of each kind have to be returned so that the company does not pay for them.

The system can produce lots of different **reports**. It can list all the types of item which have been returned and which have been found to be faulty. There is an example of this type of report in Figure 17.2. The database calculates the number of faulty items as a percentage of total sales of that item. This report shows the buying department which items are proving to be unreliable. Very unreliable items, or batches of items, can then be discontinued.

Stock_no	Description	Supplier	Total_sales	No_returned	%_returned
156	CD-ROM Drive	Marnon	45	12	26.67
15	500Mb Hard drive	Siren	678	45	6.64
18	3.5in Floppy drive	Siren	540	34	6.30
52	1Mb Simms	Exox	11789	345	2.93
3210	Display	Exox	709	6	0.85

Figure 17.2 Returned items report.

Q

Why is it important to check on staff performance?

The system will also report on staff performance as in Figure 16.3. It can print out details of each technician's work, showing how many items were tested and how often the result was wrong. This is important because customers get angry if they are told that items work properly and the fault they complained about is really still there. Suppliers of components also charge for checking components that are returned as faulty but are actually working. This means that a careless technician can cost the company a lot of money.

Technician work report

THIS REPORT IS CONFIDENTIAL

NAME: Mr. P. Jones

REPORT PRINTED ON: 30/06/95

Return_no	Stock_no	Result	Comment
12457	3210	PASS	Later tested faulty
12478	1276	FAIL	
12482	0052	FAIL	
12491	0156	FAIL	Supplier returned
12497	0156	FAIL	
12502	0018	PASS	

Figure 17.3 A staff performance report.

Another report the system produces is a list of items awaiting testing. This list is in descending order of waiting time so the item which has been waiting the longest is at the top of the list. This report is used to check that items don't get left at the back of a shelf and never get tested. When customers phone to find out what has happened to returned goods, individual records can be displayed on screen so that the person answering the phone can explain exactly what has happened to the item and when it is likely to be checked. Figure 17.4 shows a waiting time report.

Waiting time report

REPORT PRINTED ON: 30/06/95

Return_no	Order_no	Stock_no	Date_returned
10927	78965	1245	11 June 1994
12500	81179	18	27 May 1995
12502	81192	3210	27 May 1995
12503	81199	52	29 May 1995
12504	81254	156	30 May 1995
12506	81165	18	30 May 1995
12600	81287	156	02 June 1995
12601	81367	52	02 June 1995
Total items was	8		

Figure 17.4 A waiting time report.

Some customers return lots of items as faulty when they are really working. The system can list customers who have done this. Little can be done about customers who only buy one or two items, but trade customers who buy large quantities can be charged for testing if their return record is bad.

Customers returning working items

REPORT PRINTED ON: 30/06/95

Customer_no	Customer_name	Total_items	Returns	No_tested_OK	% wrong returns
96	J.Patel	2100	5	1	20.00
125	J.P Morrison	872	4	1	25.00
1195	E.T.Wheatley	235679	5426	31	0.57
1287	Bigger Computers Ltd	8546	4591	638	52.26
4532	G.D.N Associates	4256	685	54	7.88
125749	S. Kay Computers	52457	5254	2206	42.00

Figure 17.5 A report on customers returning working items.

A system like this needs good security. Much of the data is confidential and all of it is valuable to the company. Only certain users can access some of the reports. The technician performance report can be read only by the returns department manager. Individual technicians can enter some data into the system about results of tests but can't add records to the file or delete whole records. They can't edit fields which describe the item, or alter the customer or supplier data.

The only people who can actually create a returns record are the staff who receive the returned items. They can only do this when there is a valid order number and the item code is found in the order record. Customer records are added in the sales department and the returns staff can't create new customer records.

The whole system allows returns to be processed efficiently, at minimum cost to the company, and quickly enough to keep customers happy. It also helps to identify troublesome items and customers, and to check on the performance of staff.

Q

Give three reasons why the system needs good security.

18 Formula One Motor Racing

■ *McLaren*

Formula One is the peak of the sport of motor racing. It is watched by nearly half a billion people every two weeks for nine months of the year. The McLaren motor racing team have for many years enjoyed huge success. By the end of 1993, cars bearing the McLaren name had won 104 Grands Prix, making the team the most successful constructor in terms of victories in the history of Formula One. They constantly strive for excellence in their engineering and are always looking to develop new ideas which may keep them ahead of the opposition out on the track.

A McLaren Formula One racing car.

McLaren International, the Formula One racing team, is located in Woking, in the south of England, in the most advanced motor racing facility of its kind. It is made up of a 6225 square metre factory and office complex and 2415 square metre Research and Development Centre. Information Systems play a vital role in every aspect of the work of the team. Currently they have 55 computer workstations in use across the range of the team's activities.

The technical offices and the factory

McLaren have advanced **Computer Aided Design and Manufacturing (CAD/CAM)** facilities. The use of CAD in the design process is now standard in Formula One. In 1995, McLaren produced their first Formula One car which was completely designed using CAD. They had been pressing up to the 100% mark for two or three years, with around 80% of the 1993 and 1994 cars designed and built using their CAD/CAM system.

Individual components of the car can be designed, modelled and detailed on CAD either individually or together with surrounding components. They are then brought together to form sub-assemblies or can be used in an overall car model. For the first time, in 1995, McLaren used a new on-screen assembler to ensure the whole car fitted together correctly. **Concurrent Assembly Mock-Up**, or **CAMU**, manages the relationship between components, sub-assemblies and assemblies. This allows the designers to fit together components on screen, making sure that changes made to one element of the car take into account the repercussions on neighbouring parts and the whole assembly. It also allows the different engineering teams, all working on different parts of the car at the same time, to work closely, each knowing the latest state of play and giving a live model of what the other designers are working on.

Designers are able to call upon a range of modelling techniques to help them perform specific tasks. As well as being able to produce **wire-frame models** on screen (see the photograph overleaf), the CAD software allows models to show as solids and surfaces (see over). Different techniques can be applied to different components. For example, the body shape of the car will require surface modelling because of all the complex curves which fit together to make up the bodywork. But a bracket used as part of the suspension of the car may be designed as a solid, therefore taking less time to create.

Special computer programs also allow engineers to investigate different elements of design, e.g. how individual parts of a car will stand up to stress.

Studies are also made with accurate 1/3 scale models reproducing the aerodynamic features of a real car. These models are generally made of identical materials as the actual racing car, with the bodywork made of carbon fibre and the chassis, engine, gearbox and wings made of aluminium. The models also contain a wide variety of instruments and sensors that are useful when testing the design. Two types of model are produced each season: the Development Model, used to improve the performance of the current racing car and to research aerodynamic concepts, and a Replica Model produced to the exact aerodynamic configuration of the current racing car.

Q

Explain what the following initials stand for:

CAD

CAM

CAMU

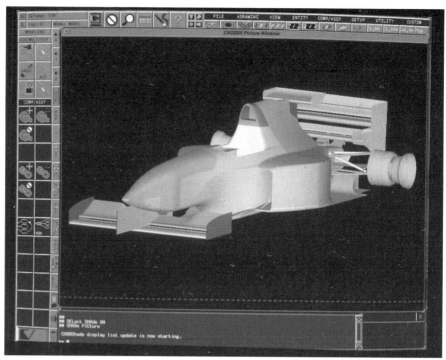

A McLaren F1 car as a 'solid' mock-up.

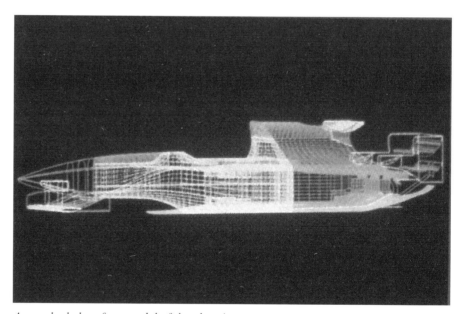

An unshaded surface model of the chassis.

Research using these models is carried out in a purpose-built wind tunnel which has a high speed rolling road to match the under-car speed with the air speed in the tunnel. This will perfectly simulate race track conditions.

Just as important as the mechanical and structural development of the racing car is that of software development. This is carried out by the Systems Engineering Department at McLaren and falls into three areas of software responsibility, detailed as follows:

CONTROL SOFTWARE

Control software deals with all functions carried out to improve the car's performance and increase safety. It runs on purpose-built multi-processor control units which are linked to the car via sensors (input) and actuators (output). These communicate with each other and the computers in the pits via special data channels. After deciding on the need to improve the performance of the car in a particular area, the systems engineers will decide on the strategy and the required sensors and actuators. Once the strategy has been approved, the software will be developed. Not only must the new software fulfil the desired functions, it must also interface with existing codes and meet all safety requirements.

MONITORING SOFTWARE

The **monitoring software** deals with the performance monitoring of the car and all the applied software strategies. All the on-board functions of the car such as sensor inputs, control inputs and many internal variables of the control software, are permanently monitored through **ATLAS (Advanced Telemetry Linked Acquisition Systems)**, which was developed by one of McLaren's sister companies. This data is stored within the control units and sent via telemetry to a computer network in the pits. **Telemetry** is the process of measuring a physical quantity and conveying its measurement over a distance using a signal.

Due to the volume of data to process, very powerful graphics workstations are required. With the help of these workstations and software developed by McLaren in-house, it is possible to analyse the performance of the car. All the information delivered by these software functions is used by the driver and the race engineers to identify problems and to perfect the performance of the cars.

SIMULATION SOFTWARE

Simulation and **modelling** are designed to understand the car's behaviour and predict how this would change if certain of its properties were modified. For example, if the suspension of the racing car can be simulated on a computer, it is possible to change various factors such as how it deals with bumps on the road without having to build it or run the actual car. One of the major uses of simulation is the set-up of the car for the next racing circuit. If certain variations of the aerodynamic set-up can be simulated on the computer, then the car can arrive at the circuit with a set-up that is already close to optimum performance.

When the design of the race car has been finalised, two more computer workstations are used in the factory to program the machine tools which make the car parts. Once assembled, it is time to take the car to the test track.

A McLaren engineer monitors track data using ATLAS.

What is telemetry ?

What three types of software were developed by the Systems Engineering Department at McLaren?

Give one example of how simulation software is used within McLaren.

At the test track

As mentioned previously, the control software for a racing car has to be developed with many adjustable parameters. These are necessary because in most cases it is not possible to predict exactly the response of the car. Only by 'tuning' these parameters can a strategy be used to its maximum performance. This happens in two steps, firstly on a test bench and then on the car itself under realistic conditions on the test track.

Bench testing includes tests to make sure the software functions as it should and tests of all the hardware components, like sensors and actuators. The complex electronics of a racing car require expensive and complicated wiring. On the 1995 McLaren, the wiring totals approximately 1000 metres. There are more than 100 **sensors**, **actuators** and **control units**, all of which need to be linked together to allow the information to flow.

The bench tests ensure that the whole system works as expected and allows for parameters to be set in such a way that, in case of any doubt, any risk can be minimised when the new function is actually tested on the car.

It is on the test track where the final and most important step of the software application is carried out. This is where, using the on-board **data-logging** and telemetry capabilities, it is possible to analyse the function of the new strategy down to one thousandth of a second.

At the test track, four workstations are dedicated to analysing the car's performance and two are dedicated to analysing the performance of the engine. Their job is to handle the data transmitted continuously back to the pits from the car about the engine and chassis parameters. As mentioned earlier, the data sent via telemetry as the car is put through its paces is transmitted via the ATLAS system to the garage, where it is then transmitted to the pits.

The data allows the engineers to analyse everything from the number of engine revolutions and oil and water pressure down to the velocity of each wheel and the steering wheel position as the car travels around the track. Together with all this performance data, the driver's feedback leads to the most favourable performance, ultimately resulting in faster lap times. If the system works safely and gives a performance improvement, it is finally ready to go from testing to racing.

At the circuit

This is what all the work has been leading up to. Most of the preparation work is complete on the cars, which can accelerate from standstill to 125mph in five seconds and have a maximum speed in the region of 211 mph.

Q

Give examples of data sent back to the pits from the racing car whilst it is on the test track.

A McLaren F1 car in action.

Computer hardware travels around the world with the team to each race point on the global circuit, in the form of five portable workstations. These provide a lap-by-lap summary of car and engine performance, again via telemetry.

Using the information read from the workstation's screens, four engineers in the pits are the only members of the team allowed to talk to the driver via a radio link to the car. This is vital in helping the drivers adjust the way they drive to take account of engine performance, oil pressure or fuel consumption. The collected data is also used to try to improve the car's performance for the next race.

Computers also record each competitor's lap timings and the race engineers can relay to a driver how far behind or in front the nearest rival is. Although there is the radio link with the car, this information is usually passed to the driver via a board as the car passes the pits. At times it may be impossible for the driver to hear as, when the engine is at full throttle, noise levels can reach 165 decibels. Despite all the computer technology, the drivers remain in charge during a race. They decide how to respond to the advice and data they are given.

Information systems play a key role in all aspects of the McLaren motor racing team and are becoming more and more sophisticated. Such is the power of the systems which have been developed that when, in 1995, a McLaren had to be redesigned as the cockpit was too cramped for Nigel Mansell, the driver, a new car was designed and built in just 33 days.

Q

Why is it important to monitor car and engine performance during a race?

19 Additional Applications

The applications in this chapter are discussed in greater detail in *This is IT!* by Anne Ramkaran and Ian Ithurralde, published by Hodder and Stoughton in 1995 (ISBN 0 340 61104 9).

■ *A Medical Centre*

A consulting room in the Medical Centre.

The Medical Centre described here is based in a small market town in the north-east of England. It is a group practice with five doctors and 9000 patients.

BEFORE COMPUTERS WERE USED

Before computers were introduced, patient's personal details were written by hand onto record cards, which were then filed away. After a patient was seen by a Doctor, details of the consultation were entered onto that patient's record card and a prescription for medicine written out by hand and given to the patient if it was needed.

As well as personal consultations the Doctors at the Centre carry out immunisations against particular diseases, follow up chronic illnesses and give advice as part of their normal procedure. Sometimes tests have to be carried out at the Centre, or samples are

Q

Describe the situation in the Medical Centre before the introduction of computers.

sent off to a hospital for analysis, and the results sent back by post. If a patient goes into hospital for any reason, notes relating to this would also have to be recorded by hand on the record cards.

INTRODUCING AN INFORMATION SYSTEM

Five years ago, the doctors decided to introduce a computer-based Information System into the practice, in order to make all areas of the medical practice run more efficiently, and therefore provide a better service to their patients.

The system has nine terminals attached to a central processor. Each terminal has its own local dot matrix printer and the fileserver, which has a removable hard disk drive used for backing up stored data, is connected to a laser printer. The software is easy to use and was written by a software house specifically for medical practices. Some of the functions of the software are used every day, others are used less often or not at all if they are not relevant to the practice.

There is now a database with a record for every patient registered at the centre. All the details from the existing record cards had to be transferred to computer database files. Using this system the doctor is also able to access two special database files. One is a conditions dictionary, which gives information about a huge range of different diseases to help make a diagnosis. The other is a drugs dictionary, which is updated every two months and contains information on all the drugs available.

When the computer system was installed in the Medical Centre, all the staff were given training. This lasted for three days and was provided by the company from whom they bought the system. This company also provided the relevant user and maintenance documentation. There then followed a six-month trial period in which both the old and new systems were run in parallel. This let the Doctors and other staff get used to the new ways of operating, as well as making sure the system worked properly.

USING THE SYSTEM

The main use of the system is to keep up-to-date records on every patient, which the doctor can look up quickly and easily.
At the end of a consultation, the Doctor enters brief details about it through the keyboard of the terminal - the date, the diagnosis and any medication prescribed. This data is stored, automatically updating the patient's computer record. If the patient needs a prescription, it can be printed out on the printer in the consulting room.

The system is used by the practice in many other ways:

Repeat prescriptions

There are times when a patient requires a repeat prescription. Each patient is now given a unique prescription number, which allows the

Q

Explain how the new computer-based system was implemented.

clerk/receptionist to identify the patient and their prescription requirements. The prescription also contains the review date for treatment and if this date has been passed, the clerk/receptionist or the Doctor can ask the patient to make an appointment for a consultation.

Communication

The computer system has improved communications with patients. For example, some patients may need to be screened (checked for a particular disease) every two years. It is possible to search the database files very quickly for every patient whose screening is due and use **mail-merging** to create letters to each of them asking them to make an appointment. This can be applied to many other situations. For example, children need to have vaccinations at particular ages and the system can produce letters to parents of children whose immunisations are due at any given time (see Figure 19.1).

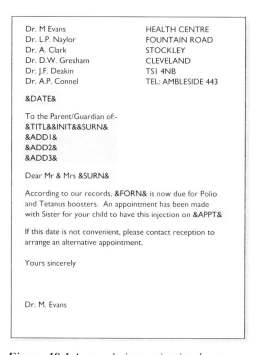

Figure 19.1 A sample immunisation letter.

In Figure 19.1 you can see a sample immunisation letter. As well as the main text which will be common to all patients, it contains codes, e.g. &TITL&, which will be replaced by items from the database file. &TITL&&INIT&&SURN& could be replaced by Miss C Smith in one letter and by Mr P N Wilson in the next.

'Drug alerts'

Sometimes it is discovered that a particular drug has negative side effects, and the Doctors need to find out which patients use, or have

Q

Explain how mail-merging is used to produce letters to patients.

Describe three procedures carried out by the Medical Centre which have been made easier since the introduction of computers.

used, the drug. The Centre can now produce very quickly accurate lists of all the patients who have used a drug. The Doctors can also use the database to produce complex reports perhaps linking the use of a particular drug to a particular side effect.

Medical research

One of the major benefits of having all this data stored electronically is that a central database can be created and used for research purposes. It contains details of diseases as well as the characteristics of the people suffering from them, the drugs and methods used to combat these conditions and details of how successful they are. About 800 medical practices provide this data and the central database file now contains medical details on over two million anonymous patients. All these practices use the same file format for the data, so that it can be easily merged together.

KEEPING THE DATA SECURE

The Medical Centre is registered as a data user with the **Data Protection Registrar** and so it follows the regulations of the **Data Protection Act** (see Chapter 14). They have safeguards against unauthorised access to the database files in their system. All the Doctors and staff each have their own **password** which they have to enter before they can use the computer system and which they change on a regular basis. All the terminals used by staff outside the consulting rooms are placed out of sight of passers-by so no-one can read patient details from the screens without permission. The system is completely contained in the building and is not connected up to the telephone lines so no-one can hack into the system from a computer outside.

It is also important to make sure that the data held on each patient is protected against accidental loss or damage so the Centre makes sure that it keeps copies of all the data, which can be used to restore the database if it ever gets corrupted. Back-up copies of the database are taken each day for this purpose on removable hard disks which are kept under lock and key in a fireproof safe. Three generations of files are kept in this way.

Explain how the Data Protection Act applies to this medical practice.

Discuss the effectiveness of the introduction of the computer system in the Medical Centre

for the patients,
for the Doctors.

FUTURE DEVELOPMENTS

Other medical practices now use systems that have been developed from the one we have looked at here. These systems are used to store, process and retrieve all patient details, including notes and comments, and there is an automatic check built in that warns if a drug about to be prescribed to a patient clashes with another drug they're already taking.

Many medical practice systems have direct communications links to hospitals via telephone lines, although this has implications in terms of security of data. With advances in communications technology, many previously unthought of practices are taking place. For example, key-hole surgery is now being carried out by surgeons who are in a different location from the patient, and uses a combination of remote links to surgical equipment and teleconferencing.

Information Systems in the Supermarket

Information systems are used widely throughout the retail industry and one area in which their use is particularly important is supermarkets. Computers are used in a variety of ways in the modern, large supermarket. Here we will concentrate on the way in which systems are used for stock control and control of fridges and freezers in one particular large supermarket, which is part of a national chain.

STOCK CONTROL

The system office.

The supermarket uses several computers which are located in a room known as the system office, which you can see in the photograph (above). One of these computers is used to control the stock and is connected to each checkout. We shall call this the branch computer. Located at each checkout is an **Electronic Point Of Sale (EPOS)** till. This comprises a keyboard, a digital display, a scanner which reads bar codes, a set of scales, a printer, a credit/debit card reader and a till drawer. Each till also has its own base to which

Figure 19.2 An EAN barcode.

Q

Describe the process by which bar codes are used to obtain the price and description of a product.

all of the above is attached. This base unit is connected by cables to the branch computer in the supermarket's system office.

Each product to be sold must have an identifying code number which is different from that of every other product. Different sizes of the same product even need different code numbers. These code numbers are printed onto the labels or packaging of the product in the form of **bar codes**.

Bar codes are made up of a set of black lines and white spaces. Look at the bar code in Figure 19.2. You can see that it is split into two halves, and each half is contained within two thin black stripes which are slightly longer than the rest.

Figure 19.3 shows the pattern of lines for the digits 2 and 7. Notice that the pattern for a digit on the right hand half of a bar code is the opposite of the one on the left hand half.

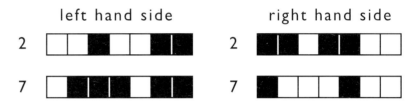

Figure 19.3 Bar code patterns for the digits 2 and 7.

Many bar codes today use the **European Article Number** or **EAN**. This is a thirteen digit number which can be used to uniquely identify a product. Using the bar code shown in Figure 19.2 as an example, we can see what the various parts of the number mean.

- The first two digits represent the country from which the company producing the product comes. In this example 50 denotes the UK.

- The next five digits represent the company which produced the product. 00208 is for Lyons Tetley Ltd.

- The following five digits represent the product. 02100 means 80 tea bags.

- The last number is the check digit. This is used to make sure that the bar code has been read correctly.

So 5000208021000 is the EAN for a box of 80 Tetley tea bags.

The bar codes on products are read by the EPOS tills at the checkouts. This is achieved by using a **scanner**, which sends out infra-red laser beams via a set of mirrors, enabling the bar code to be read at most angles.

When an item is passed over the scanner, the black and white parts of the code are detected by the laser, as the black parts reflect very little light whilst the white parts reflect most of the light. This is converted into electrical pulses which are sent along the cables to the branch computer. You can see how the system is set up in Figure

19.4. The branch computer then searches its stock file for the product matching the EAN number. When this record is located, the price and description of the product is extracted and sent back to the EPOS till at the checkout which then shows this item and price on the digital display, prints them on a receipt and adds the price to the total. At the same time, the branch computer records that one unit of this item has been sold. This whole process is shown in Figure 19.5.

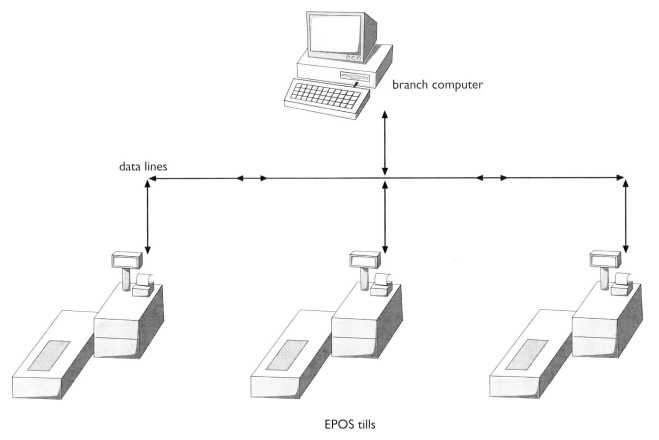

Figure 19.4 *The branch computer is connected to the EPOS tills.*

The scales at the EPOS till are also linked up to the branch computer. All loose fruit and vegetables are weighed at the checkout. Each product has a code number which, when typed in at the keyboard, gives the customer a description of the product on the receipt along with the weight and price of the purchase. The weight of the product is also deducted from the stock file.

There are, in fact, two branch computers linked to the EPOS terminals at the checkouts. They both record information about items sold and provide back-up for each other. If only one computer was used and it broke down, the supermarket could not function.

These branch computers are linked via the telephone lines to a large main computer housed at the supermarket's head office elsewhere in the country. All branches of this supermarket are also linked by phone to the main computer.

Q

What does the abbreviation EPOS stand for?

List the components which make up an EPOS till.

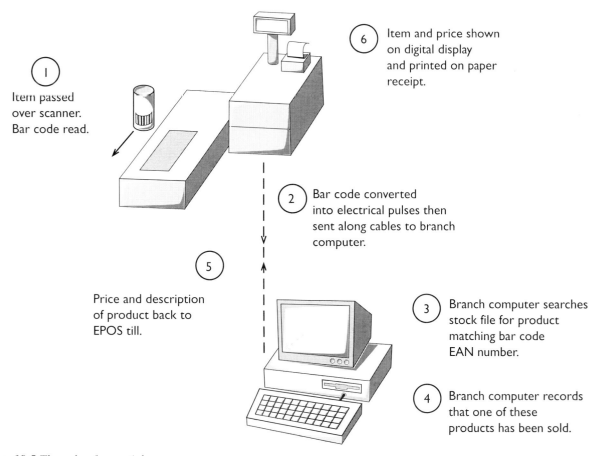

Figure 19.5 *The sale of an article.*

After the supermarket has closed at the end of the day, the following happens:

1   The branch computer sends the details of every individual sale to the main computer at the Head Office.

2   Using this information, the main computer system updates its record of the number in stock of every item in the store.

3   Using a forecast of sales along with other factors, such as the weather and the time of the year, the system automatically orders the correct amount of stock required by the store for the next day.

4   The main computer also transmits these orders to computers in the distribution centres (large warehouses storing products ready for delivery to stores) via the telephone lines.

5   These distribution centres then send the required stock by road to the stores immediately.

6   Price changes and prices of new products, special offers, etc. are sent back to the branch computer in the supermarket.

7   New shelf labels are printed and the night staff at the supermarket place these on the shelves ready for the following day.

Q

Describe the steps involved in the process of stock control in the supermarket.

You can see this process summarised in Figure 19.6.

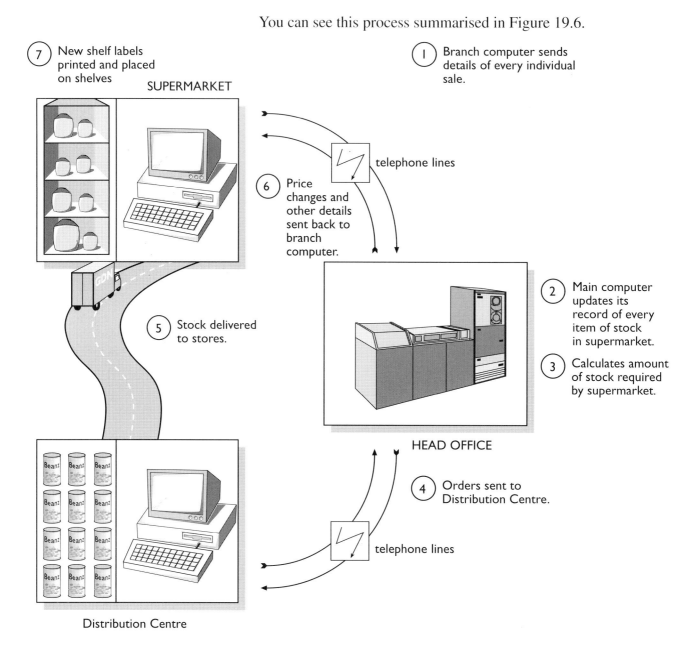

Figure 19.6 The process of stock control.

CONTROL SYSTEMS

Computers are also used to control the freezers and chillers throughout the store. In the warehouse, the large freezers have to be kept within a certain temperature range. This is achieved by having temperature sensors inside each freezer which monitor the conditions and switch the cooling motor on or off.

On the floor of the supermarket are many freezers and chillers which are used to store and display a wide variety of products such as fresh meat, dairy produce and frozen goods. Different products have different requirements in terms of temperature. Fresh meat, for

Outline two ways in which computer systems are used in the supermarket.

instance, may have to be kept at 4 °C whilst ice cream has to be stored at -15 °C. The freezers and chillers therefore are kept at many different temperatures and, in the past, an employee of the supermarket had to check the temperature of the chiller every hour. Now every freezer and chiller is linked to a computer in the branch office. A temperature sensor in each freezer or chiller constantly monitors the temperature, sending data back to this computer. The computer sends signals back, when needed, switching the individual freezer or chiller motors on or off, thus maintaining the correct temperatures. A display on each freezer or chiller shows the temperature to customers.

This is called a **closed loop control system**. As can be seen in Figure 19.7, the freezer can be either on or off (the process) which leads to the freezer reaching a certain temperature (the result). The temperature of the freezer is then either too high, too low or all right and this feedback is used to change the process, if necessary, by turning the freezer from off to on or on to off.

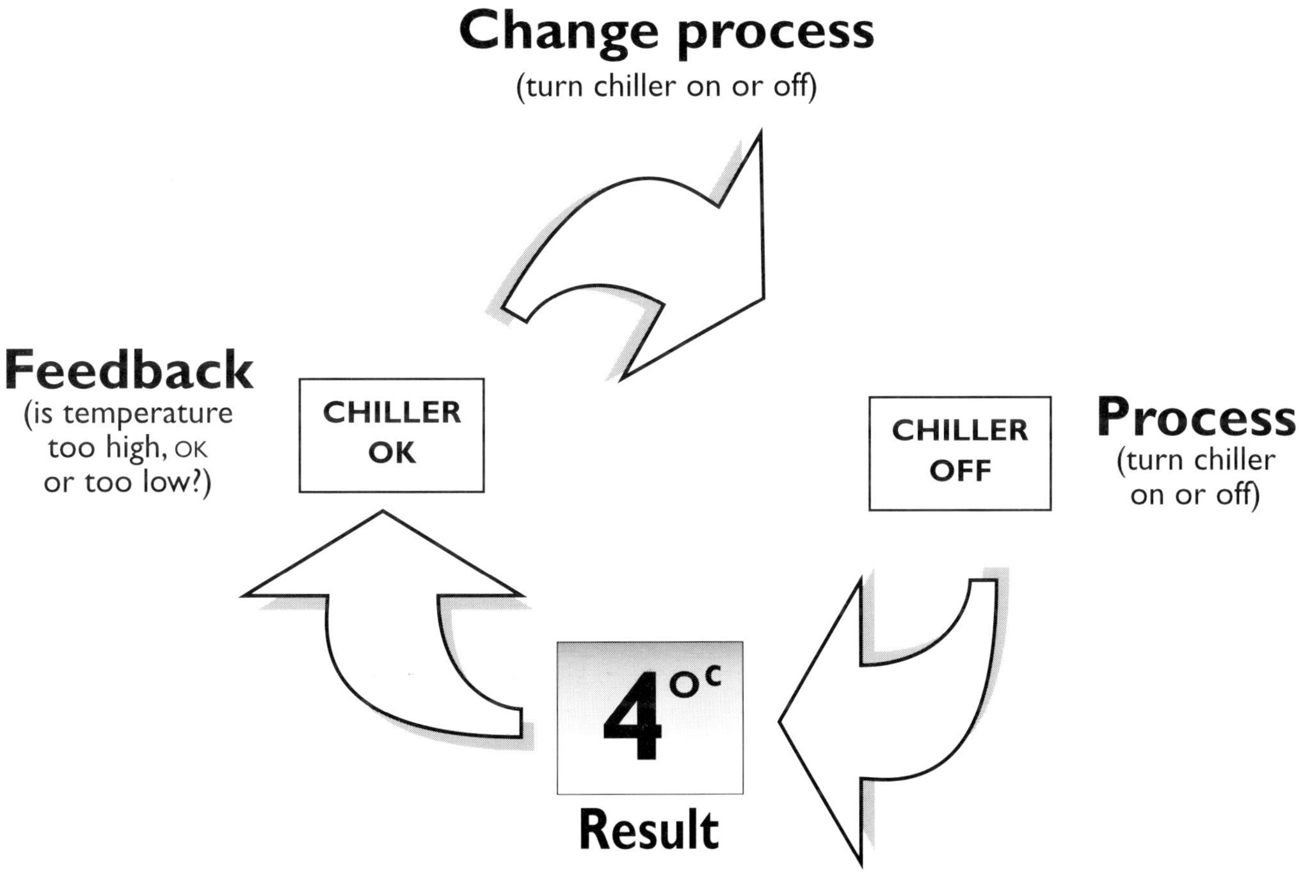

Change process
(turn chiller on or off)

Feedback
(is temperature too high, OK or too low?)

| CHILLER OK |

| CHILLER OFF |

Process
(turn chiller on or off)

$4 \, °C$

Result

Figure 19.7 A closed loop control system.

Every three or four hours, each freezer has to be defrosted and the computer controls this process as well, turning the freezer off long enough to stop the build up of ice but without defrosting the food. Any breakdowns are detected immediately, minimising the risk of food thawing and therefore being wasted.

Q

What is meant by a closed loop control system?

Explain how monitoring and control are used within the supermarket.

Stock control and the maintenance of freezers and chillers are only two of the ways in which computers are used within the supermarket industry. They have been introduced to produce benefits for both the customer and the supermarket management.

It must be remembered that changes and improvements come about over a long period of time. For instance, while the introduction of Information Systems may save the supermarket chain money eventually, it requires a good deal of investment, both in terms of resources and training, initially and throughout its development.

An Urban Traffic Control System

In this section we are going to look at the urban traffic control system that is in operation in the towns of Middlesbrough and Stockton-on-Tees in the county of Cleveland.

Q

Describe an urban traffic control system in your own words.

WHAT IS AN URBAN TRAFFIC CONTROL SYSTEM?

An urban traffic control system operates the traffic lights at road junctions and pedestrian crossings and controls the flow of traffic along these roads. The system we will be looking at here has three ways of operating the traffic lights and pedestrian crossings, which work at different times of the day.

Vehicle-activated mode

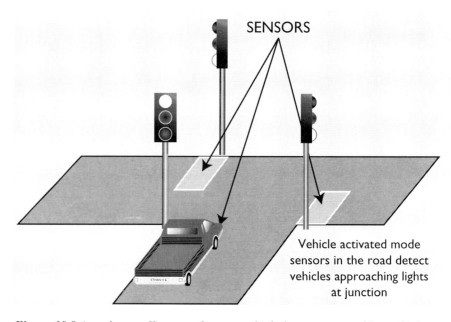

SENSORS

Vehicle activated mode sensors in the road detect vehicles approaching lights at junction

Figure 19.8 An urban traffic control system which detects approaching vehicles.

Describe the way the system works when in vehicle activated mode.

Traffic lights at a junction work as a set. During the evening they operate in vehicle-activated mode. Sensors built into the road near the junction detect when a vehicle is approaching the lights (see Figure 19.8). If the lights are already on green for that vehicle then the lights won't change but, if they are on red, they will change to green. The lights for the other roads entering the junction have to be changed first (see Figure 19.9).

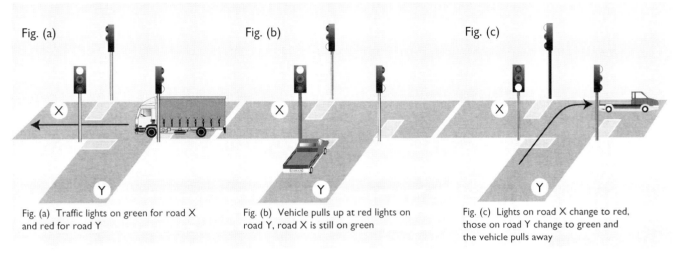

Fig. (a)   Fig. (b)   Fig. (c)

Fig. (a) Traffic lights on green for road X and red for road Y

Fig. (b) Vehicle pulls up at red lights on road Y, road X is still on green

Fig. (c) Lights on road X change to red, those on road Y change to green and the vehicle pulls away

Figure 19.9 A vehicle-activated traffic light system.

Fixed time mode

If the traffic flow gets heavier, the vehicle-activated mode causes problems because the lights are changed too often. The system then switches to fixed time mode. At each junction, a microprocessor contains a number of different plans to control the timing of the sequence of lights. The particular plan used depends upon the time of day. The fixed time plans determine how long each part of the cycle of lights for each traffic light at the junction will last. You can see one of the plans in Figure 19.10.

The amount of time the lights stay at point 1 and point 5 depends on the plan, and the plan is based on a prediction of the average traffic flow through the junction at that particular time of day. The four plans used in Cleveland are:

What is meant by fixed time mode?

Why are fixed time plans needed?

What are the four fixed time plans used in Cleveland?

How were these timings calculated?

• Peak a.m.
• Off-peak a.m.
• Peak p.m.
• Off-peak p.m.

The timings used in these plans were worked out using traffic surveys, then the times were programmed into the microprocessors at the junctions. These microprocessors, using the clock built into them, then select the correct plan for the time of day.

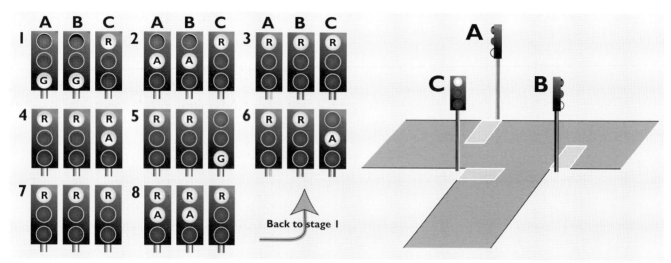

Figure 19.10 Fixed time plans.

Program controlled

What is controlled in program controlled mode?

Describe how the central computer calculates the flow of traffic at any particular junction.

The third method is computer-controlled operation. Since 1985 the traffic lights and pelican crossings in the central areas of both Middlesbrough and Stockton-on-Tees have been controlled between 7a.m. and 7p.m. by a central computer sited in one of the County Council's offices in Middlesbrough.

There are 42 junctions and 22 pelican crossings under the central computer's control. On each road leading to a junction that is controlled using this system, and at some distance from that junction, a detector is buried in the road. Every time a vehicle passes over this detector it sends a signal along a dedicated telephone line to the central computer (see Figure 19.11). The computer knows the colour of the lights at that time and the average speed of a vehicle between the detector and the junction, and so can calculate the rate of flow of traffic for each road in and out of that junction.

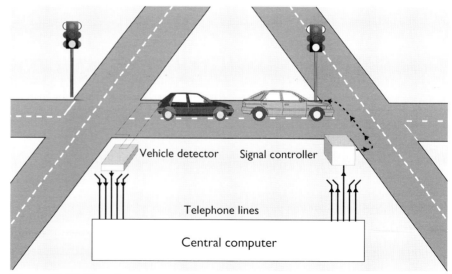

Figure 19.11 How the system works.

At any time the state of the flow of traffic can be displayed on a screen in the control room in the County Council Office. Although these displays allow the traffic controller to see exactly what is happening in great detail, the computer program, not the controller, actually deals with the problems of congestion. The program takes into account all the data being fed into it, and tries to relieve the queues and congestion by altering, a little at a time, the timings of the lights.

The computer uses a technique called SCOOT (this stands for Split Cycle Offset Optimisation Technique), and the program in the central computer can alter the time any light is on a particular colour (the split), the time it takes for a set of lights to go through a complete cycle (the cycle) and the timings between different junctions (the offset). The controller can change the timings manually, but doesn't do it very often, usually only when accidents occur or when there are roadworks in the area.

Q

Give a reason why the controller might have to change the timings manually.

WHAT HAPPENS IF THE SYSTEM FAILS?

If the computer system fails, the traffic lights automatically go back to operating in fixed time mode. If faults occur, the condition shows up on the various screen displays and a buzzer sounds in the control room. These faults are logged by the computer and can be printed out at any time. At 3a.m. the computer program checks all parts of the system (detectors, lights, etc.) for faults and the results of these tests are logged and printed out so that the engineers can trace any faults and repair them.

Q

Describe what happens if the computer-controlled system breaks down.

CAR PARKING

This computer system also controls the information signs about car parks in the town centre. Detectors in the road at the entrances and exits of the car parks send signals back to the central computer which can then count the number of vehicles in each car park. The computer also stores the total number of vehicles each car park can accommodate and sends signals to the electronic signs to display each car park's status, such as whether it has spaces, how full it is or whether it is closed. Two systems of car park monitoring can be seen in Figures 19.12 and 19.13.

Diagrams displayed on the monitor in the offices can show the details of all the car parks in an area or details of each car park separately. These displays give the status, the capacity of the car park, the number of vehicles currently parked and the number of faulty detectors. The screen for one particular car park also shows the message that's being displayed on electronic information signs in the area, regarding its state. Exactly what is being displayed on each of these signs can also be shown on the screen. You can see one of these displays in Figure 19.14 and the sign the drivers see below it.

Q

Describe how the computer system monitors parking in the town centre car parks.

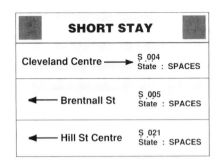

Figure 19.14 *The screen showing the display on the car park sign.*

The actual sign.

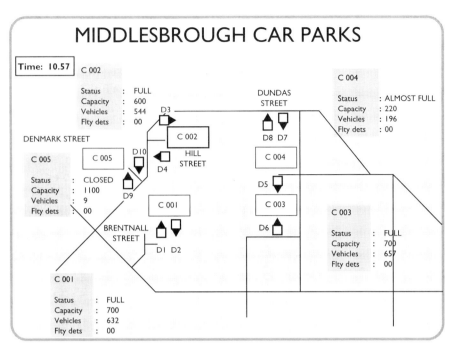

Figure 19.12 *Car park monitoring.*

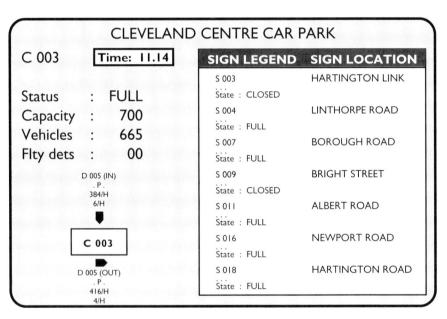

Figure 19.13 *Another display used to monitor car parks.*

Examination Questions

All of the following questions are taken from GCSE papers set in June 1995.

The first section of questions is designed to refresh pupils on subjects covered in *This is IT!*. The subject order of the remaining questions follows approximately the order of chapters in the book and have been divided into sections on this basis. Many questions involve more than one topic and have been grouped together separately at the end. These will be especially useful for revision purposes.

Refresher questions

1 Describe TWO advantages of storing and processing data using information technology methods compared with traditional methods such as a card index.

City and Guilds

2 From the list of packages given, choose the best one for each of the applications below.

CAD
Communications
Database
Desk Top Publishing (DTP)
Spreadsheet

a) Producing a school magazine

b) Designing a kitchen layout

c) Storing details of all the books in a library   *(3 marks)*
NEAB

3 GoSun travel agency arranges day trips. This is a fax to the station manager at Nelson Railway station.

> **FAX**
> To: The station manager, Nelson railway station.
> From: GoSun travel agency.
>
> On 1/7/95 at 8.00 am, there will be a day trip by train from Nelson to Blackpool. The return fare is £3.50. Please arrange local advertising.

The station manager has asked you to design a poster to advertise this day trip.

a) Explain why the fax itself is not suitable for advertising the day trip. *(2 marks)*

b) From the list, write down TWO forms of information that could be in the poster.

formulae
pictures
graphs
sound
words *(2 marks)*

c) Give TWO reasons why Desk Top Publishing (DTP) software may be better than a word processor for producing a poster. *(2 marks)*

d) You can print the poster on one of these printers.

daisy wheel
dot matrix
laser

   (i) From the list write down the type of printer that would produce the best black and white poster. *(1 mark)*
   (ii) Give a reason for your choice. *(1 mark)*

e) GoSun keeps the information about all its day trips on a database. This is part of the database:

TRIP NUMBER	FROM	TO	DATE	TRANSPORT
027	Leeds	Chester	27/10/95	Rail
369	Watford	Bradford	01/01/96	Bus
041	Guildford	Plymouth	14/12/95	Rail
333	Colchester	Plymouth	16/11/95	Rail
502	St Ives	London	02/03/96	Bus
691	Leeds	London	11/09/95	Rail
413	London	Reading	11/09/95	Rail

(i) Each line is part of a record. Write down the number of fields shown from each record. *(1 mark)*

(ii) Write down the name of the field that identified the record. *(1 mark)*

(iii) Write down the **Trip Number** of the day trips selected by these search conditions:

Search condition 1: **Date** is 14/12/95
Search condition 2: **Trip Number** is more than 600.
Search condition 3: **Transport** is rail and **To** is London. *(3 marks)*

(iv) State TWO more fields that should be included in each record. *(2 marks)*

(v) Complete the sentences using terms from the list.

amend
delete
insert
search
sort

You remove a record from the database when you -------------------- the record.
You add another record to the database when you -------------------- the record.
The records are arranged in the order you asked for when you ------------------------ the field.
You change the data in a field when you ------------------------ the field. *(4 marks)*

(vi) Explain why the database should be a direct access file. *(2 marks)*

(vii) GoSun has 800 day trips on the database. Give TWO advantages to GoSun in using the database instead of writing down the information about day trips. *(2 marks)*

Total marks - 23
SEG

4 An information system is needed for a museum. The system will store data on all the objects the museum owns and will be able to produce various reports about objects, their history and their location. The system could be set up either using a database package or by writing a program in a suitable computer language.

a) Give three advantages of using a database package for this application. *(3 marks)*

b) Give one advantage of writing a program for this application. *(1 mark)*

NEAB

5 A newsagent wants to store details of orders for papers on his computer system. He would like to print a delivery list for each paper round and also to print lists of people who have not paid their bills.

a) What kind of package would be used to set up this system?

(1 mark)

b) Give two reasons why this kind of package would be best.

(2 marks)

c) List four pieces of information that would need to be stored.

(4 marks)

NEAB

6 A tyre manufacturer uses a computer-based model to work out stopping distances for cars.

a) Give TWO reasons why a car manufacturer would use a computer-based model. *(2 marks)*

b) Three of these rules should be built into the model. Tick THREE boxes to show the rules that should be built into the model. *(3 marks)*

Rule	Tick THREE boxes
A car travelling at high speed takes longer to stop than a car travelling at slow speed.	
Motorway driving can be very boring.	
A car with faulty brakes takes longer to stop than a car with good brakes.	
Heavier cars use more petrol.	
Cars take longer to stop on a wet road than on a dry road.	
Red cars are more visible than grey cars.	

c) You are asked to design a computer-based model to work out the stopping distances of cars. One factor that will need to be considered is the condition of the tyres. Identify THREE factors that will affect stopping distance once braking has started.

(3 marks)

d) Two of the following developments may lead to the rules built into the model being changed. Tick TWO boxes to show the developments that may lead to the rules being changed.

Development	Tick TWO boxes
Side impact bars are built into car doors.	
Petrol prices come down.	
The brakes fitted to cars are improved.	
Cars have more reliable engines.	
Tyre tread design is changed.	

Total marks - 10

SEG

Chapters 1 & 2

7 A computer system is made up of hardware and software.

a) Label the diagram using the words listed.

disc drive   display unit   icons
mouse   numeric keyboard   pointer
pull-down menu   scroll bar   window   *(4 marks)*

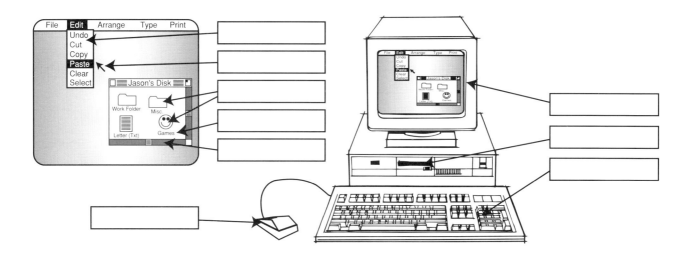

b) (i) Describe how you would use the above equipment to create a new simple ticket for your school play. The ticket needs to include the school badge. *(5 marks)*
    (ii) Name the missing piece of hardware. *(1 mark)*

Total marks - 10
MEG

8 a) Complete the table below.

Most suitable output device	Application
Producing large plans for an architect.	
Producing a school magazine.	
Producing receipts with carbon copies.	
Producing a warning when a bar code is read wrongly.	

(4 marks)

b) The immediate access store (IAS) of a computer system includes both ROM and RAM.

    (i)   Explain the meaning of

        ROM

        RAM   *(2 marks)*

    (ii) Why are both needed?   *(2 marks)*

NEAB

9

a) Name THREE different peripheral devices.

b) Suggest an appropriate application where each of the answers in a) could be used.

City and Guilds

10 A   Keyboard

      B   Screen (VDU)

      C   Mouse

      D   Printer

      E   Joystick

Which two of these are output devices?   *(2 marks)*

NEAB

Chapter 3

Questions with parts on OMR, MICR, bar codes and sensors can be found in the applications and multi-topic questions at the end.

Chapter 4

11 Some software packages are supplied as compressed files on floppy disks. Give two advantages and two disadvantages of supplying software in this way.   *(4 marks)*

NEAB

12 Each complete page of a newspaper is approximately 600 Mb in size. A standard double density floppy disk can store 720 Kb.

a) Explain what the term megabyte (MB) means.

b) How many floppy disks would be needed to store one page?

City and Guilds

13 CD-ROMs are now used to store computer games. Give THREE advantages and ONE disadvantage of supplying games on CD-ROM rather than on floppy disk. *(4 marks)*

NEAB

Chapter 6

Part of multi-topic question 36 concerns printers.

Chapter 7

Questions 37 in the multi-topic section has parts on topics in this chapter.

Chapter 8

Multi-topic questions 34, 35 and 41 have parts relevant to this chapter.

Chapter 9

14

a) Describe the term batch processing.

b) Suggest a suitable application for batch processing.

City and Guilds

See also question 49 in the multi-topic section.

Chapter 11

15 A national newspaper links its various departments using both LANs and WANs.

a) What does the term LAN mean?

b) Describe how it would be used by the newspaper group.

City and Guilds

See also questions 42 and 44 in the multi-topic section.

Chapters 13 and 14

16 Errors in some data stored on computer may cause long-term damage to individuals or organisations.

a) (i) Suggest TWO such errors that might affect an individual.
(2 marks)

(ii) Choose ONE of your answers in (i) and state what the effect may be. *(1 mark)*

b) Suggest how an individual could be compensated for ONE of the errors described in a). *(2 marks)*

City and Guilds

17 Mail order companies store personal data about their customers on computer files. The Data Protection Act is designed to protect customers from data misuse.

a) Give THREE rights that this Act gives to the customer.
(3 marks)

b) Accidental damage to or loss of data has to be prevented. Describe THREE precautions that data-users should take to try to stop this from happening. *(3 marks)*

NEAB

Several multi-topic questions also contain parts on data security and data law.

Chapter 15

18 Describe the methods used to test software in a system.

City and Guilds

19 A problem has been analysed and a specification has been produced for development of a computer-based solution. Describe each of the following stages of the development of this system.

a) Designing the solution,

b) Implementing the solution,

c) Testing the solution. *(8 marks)*

NEAB

20 The owners of a chain of video shops are considering using a computer system to handle stock records and loans of videos. You are asked to produce a feasibility report.

a) Describe three ways in which you could find out about the existing system. *(6 marks)*

b) As a result of this study you are asked to design a new computerised system. Give THREE items the design should include. *(3 marks)*

c) When the new system is installed a User Guide is provided for the shop staff. Describe THREE topics you would expect to be covered in this guide. *(3 marks)*

d) When the system is installed the staff may not be able to use it straight away. Give two reasons why they might not be able to switch to the new system immediately. *(2 marks)*

NEAB

21 The use of IT is now commonplace at many sporting events (such as international athletics meetings).

a) Describe the effects IT has had on the recording and reporting of results. *(6 marks)*

b) Describe how the organisers of a sporting event can assess the effectiveness of a computerised system before using it at an event. *(6 marks)*

City and Guilds

22 Three types of user interface are:

Diagram A	Diagram B	Diagram C

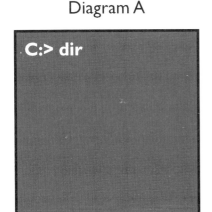

Command Driven

Menu
1. Add record
2. Delete record
3. Amend record
4. Print reports
5. Quit
Choose one of these

Menu Driven

Graphical

a) Give one reason why an inexperienced user might find the command driven interface in Diagram A difficult to use.

(1 mark)

b) Give two reasons why a user might find the graphical interface in Diagram C easier to use. *(2 marks)*

c) The menu driven interface shown in diagram B is still used for many applications. Describe one advantage to the user of this interface compared with the graphical interface shown in Diagram C. *(2 marks)*

d) At present a firm has software with a menu driven user interface. It is proposed that their system is replaced with software using a graphical user interface. Discuss the implications of making this change. *(10 marks)*

NEAB

Multi-topic questions 37 and 38 also contain parts on documentation.

Chapter 16

23 Name THREE benefits and THREE problems experienced by customers that are due to the increased use of information technology by banks. *(3 marks)*

City and Guilds

24
a) When a cash machine is used to withdraw money from a bank account, the person puts his card into the machine and enters his number.
(i) Explain why he has to type in his number. *(1 mark)*
(ii) How is data stored on the card? *(2 marks)*

b) A customer writes a cheque to pay for goods. The shop sends the cheque to its own bank.
(i) What information on the cheque has to be encoded before the data can be read by an input device. *(1 mark)*
(ii) Why do banks use this method rather than other methods to input the data? *(1 mark)*

NEAB

25 MICR is an important technology in banking. What does the term MICR mean? Briefly describe how it works. *(3 marks)*

City and Guilds

26 Study Fig. I below showing a sample cheque.

```
┌─────────────────────────────────────────────────────────────────────┐
│  SPECIMEN                                    19            44-04-36    │
│                                                                       │
│  UNITED                                                               │
│        21 The Grange, Ashstowe, Kent.                                 │
│                                                              or order  │
│  Pay _____                                 │
│                                           A  P          ┌───────────┐ │
│      _____    C  A          │ £         │ │
│                                           C  Y          └───────────┘ │
│                                           O  E                         │
│      _____    U  E            S.P.Arney     │
│                                           N                            │
│                                           T                            │
│                                                                       │
│    ꞮꞮˈ100151ꞮꞮˈ  77··0506ꞮꞮ:  04207160ꞮꞮˈ                              │
└─────────────────────────────────────────────────────────────────────┘
```
Fig. 1

a) The bottom line of the above cheque is written in MICR characters. State TWO advantages of using an MICR machine for processing cheques.   *(2 marks)*

b) State ONE limitation of using this machine.   *(1 mark)*

c) The pre-printed data on the bottom of the cheque does not include the value of the cheque. Describe ONE manual and ONE automated (IT) method that the local bank branch might use to add the value to the cheque, and suggest ONE advantage for each method.   *(4 marks)*

City and Guilds

Chapter 17

27 Mail order companies store personal data about their customers on computer files. The Data Protection Act is designed to protect customers from data misuse.

a) Give three rights that this Act gives to the customer. *(3 marks)*

b) Give five requirements concerning data that the company must meet to comply with the act.   *(5 marks)*

c) Some data is not covered by the Data Protection Act. Name one category of data which is granted complete exemption from the Act.   *(1 mark)*

NEAB

Chapter 19

28 Many medical practices and health centres now store patient information on computer files.

a) Name three items of personal information (other than name and address) that could be stored. *(3 marks)*

b) Patients may be worried about people gaining unauthorised access to these files. Give THREE ways of preventing this. *(3 marks)*

c) In a particular health centre, a local area network (LAN) is used, providing terminals and local printers in each of the doctors' rooms.

Give TWO advantages of this network instead of using stand alone machines in each doctor's room. *(2 marks)*

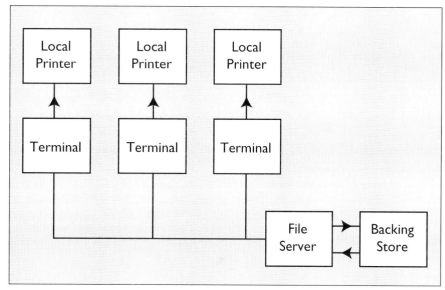

d) It is proposed to link the network in all the surgeries and health centres in the area to the main hospital computer system to form a wide area network (WAN).
   (i) Name an extra device that will be needed in the surgery to allow the connection to be made. *(1 mark)*
   (ii) What is the function of this device? *(1 mark)*

e) For each of the following give an example of data which:
   (i) might be transmitted from a doctor in a surgery to the hospital, *(1 mark)*
   (ii) might be transmitted from the hospital to the doctor. *(1 mark)*

NEAB

29 A supermarket uses a point of sale (POS) system. All the products sold carry bar codes.

a) Name the device used to input bar code data at the tills.

(1 mark)

b) The bar code contains a check digit. Explain how this would be used to detect an error in reading the bar code. *(3 marks)*

c) Give two advantages of a point of sale (POS) system compared with a manual system:
(i) For the shopper,

(ii) For the supermarket manager. *(4 marks)*

NEAB

30 Study Fig. 1 below of an EFT-POS network (showing the remote links between the retailer's computer, the bank and the EFT-POS packet switching computers).
What are the advantages of EFT-POS to the customer and the retailer? *(2 marks)*

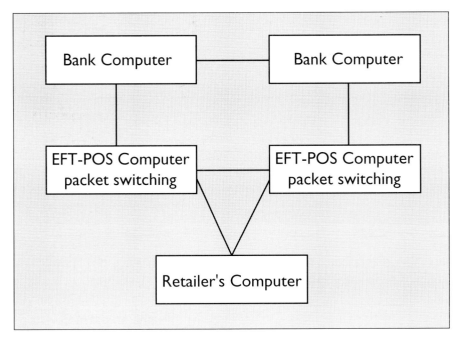

Fig. 1

City and Guilds

31 What security measures are taken to protect EFT-POS systems? *(2 marks)*

City and Guilds

32 Explain why EFT-POS transactions must use real-time processing.

(3 marks)

City and Guilds

33 A supermarket has several point-of-sale (POS) checkouts connected to a mini-computer in the same building. All supermarkets have bar codes on their labels.

a) Explain how a bar code is automatically read and accepted at a checkout. *(2 marks)*

b) Describe how each bar code is validated. *(2 marks)*

c) Prices are not shown on most of the bar codes. Give a reason for this. *(1 mark)*

d) Some customers pay for their shopping using EFTPOS (Electronic Funds Transfer at Point Of Sale). Explain how this method of payment works. *(4 marks)*

e) Details of daily sales are stored on the minicomputer. At the end of each day this data needs to be sent to another computer at Head Office many miles away. Describe how this transfer takes place. *(3 marks)*

MEG

Multi-topic questions

34

data	field	floppy disk	RAM
validation	verification	virus	VDU

Find the best word in the above list to complete each sentence below.

a) ----------------- is a type of computer memory.

b) ----------------- is checking that data is sensible.

c) A ---------------- is a part of a record.

d) A computer system can get a ---------------------- on its hard disk. This may damage the ---------------------- stored on the disk. *(5 marks)*

NEAB

35 A government computer stores data about cars and their owners. Some of this data is shown below.

a) Using suitable examples from the data given below, explain the meaning of the terms field, file and record.

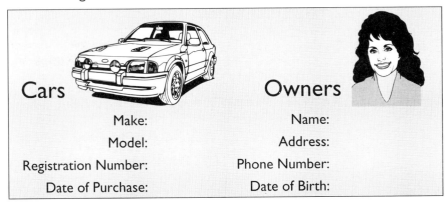

Cars

Make:

Model:

Registration Number:

Date of Purchase:

Owners

Name:

Address:

Phone Number:

Date of Birth:

b) Describe how the data should be tested for accuracy.

MEG

36

a) Mr Williams, the Headteacher, uses a spreadsheet to help him decide how to allocate amounts of money to different areas of the school. When Mr Williams first uses his spreadsheet program, he enters details about each of the areas he needs to allocate the money to. One of his first concerns is that he does not exceed the budget he has been given.

(i) Describe how the data concerning the amounts of money allocated should be stored by the program. *(1 mark)*

(ii) Describe how the spreadsheet could be used to total these amounts. *(2 marks)*

(iii) Illustrate your answer with a suitable screen representation showing the formula. *(2 marks)*

Mr Williams can use his spreadsheet to model and compare the amount of money allocated with school outgoings each month.

(iv) Describe and justify ONE possible action he could take if one area spent too much and another too little. *(2 marks)*

b) Mr Black, the Deputy Headteacher, uses an old microcomputer, 5 1/4 inch floppy disks and an Epson dot matrix printer to record examination entries for the school. The program he is using has long since been updated but he continues to use an old version which suits his equipment. When he gathers information he writes this down on odd bits of paper, often making mistakes.

(i) Give ONE reason why the methods used by Mr Black at present may not be appropriate for each of the following:

hardware
software
data capture   *(3 marks)*

(ii) Explain why Mr Black's use of information technology is preferable to manual methods of each of the following:

speed
quality of presentation
accuracy   *(3 marks)*

(iii) Give TWO advantages to the school of using an up-to-date computerised examination entry program.   *(2 marks)*

c) Mr Black has recently received details of how he can send his information entries direct via the telephone lines, to a central base which will distribute the examination entries to each relevant examination board.

(i)   Give TWO reasons why this method of transmitting the examination entries in appropriate.   *(2 marks)*

(ii) State TWO possible disadvantages to the school of using this method to send its examination entries.   *(2 marks)*

(iii) Give ONE advantage of using the computerised examination entry system to search and sort examination entry data for various heads of department, compared to manual methods.   *(1 mark)*

(iv) Describe TWO print-outs that Mr Black should be able to produce.   *(2 marks)*

d) Mr Black has been using and old microcomputer, 51/4 inch floppy disk and a 9-pin dot matrix printer to record examination entries for the school.

(i)   Critically comment on each of these items for the purpose of Mr Black's task and suggest how each could be upgraded in order to make his task more efficient.   *(6 marks)*

Mr Black would like to speed up his initial data capture by using data capture forms.

(ii) Comment on his present system with regard to the intended use of data entry forms.   *(2 marks)*

(iii) Identify TWO improvements which he could consider in order to make his system of data capture more efficient.   *(2 marks)*

Total marks - 32.

RSA

37 Some people live a long way from the shops. A grocer uses a mobile shop to sell groceries to these customers. The grocer uses a spreadsheet to keep a record of sales.

a) The grocer uses this computer system to run the spreadsheet. Complete the table by writing Input, Output or Backing Store next to each hardware device. *(5 marks)*

Hardware Device	Write Input, Output or Backing Store next to each hardware device
Disk drive	
Keyboard	
Monitor	
Mouse	
Printer	

b) Complete the sentences using terms from the list.

bar code
format
memory
operating system
turnaround document

The grocer switches on the computer. The --------------------------- loads and runs automatically.
The grocer uses the operating system to ------------------------- a floppy disk.

c) This is the spreadsheet showing sales on Tuesday.

	A	B	C	D	E
1	Tuesday	16/5/95			
2					
3	Description	Unit	Number sold	Price	Sales value
4	Apples	kg	6	0.70	4.20
5	Potatoes	25kg	9	6.00	54.00
6	Oranges	kg	9	0.90	8.10
7	Mangoes	singles	8	0.80	6.40
8	Lychees	kg	2	3.20	6.40
9	Carrots	25kg sack	8	8.50	68.00
10					
11				Total is	147.120

(i) The word 'Apples' is in cell A4. Write down the contents of cell B7. *(1 mark)*

(ii) Complete the sentence using the terms from the list.

a fax
a formula
a microprocessor
a number
a word processor
words

A cell in a spreadsheet can contain ----------------------------
----
or ---

(iii) If the number in cell C5 is changed, the number in cell E5 changes automatically. What is contained in cell E5?

(1 mark)

The number in another cell should change automatically. What is the cell reference of this cell? *(1 mark)*

d) The grocer has some documentation for the spreadsheet. Tick THREE boxes to show the sections that should be in the documentation. *(3 marks)*

Section	Tick THREE boxes
A tutorial guide to help the grocer use the spreadsheet.	
An index to help the grocer find the information.	
A lesson on percentages in case the grocer has forgotten how to do them.	
A road map to help the grocer find the route.	
A section on how to install the spreadsheet.	
A dictionary so that the grocer can look up the meaning of words.	

e) Describe TWO advantages to the grocer in using a spreadsheet instead of writing the information on paper. *(2 marks)*

> F3 changes the data directory to that of the displayed current directory of the previously current directory. The data directory is the default and is keepable (using GLOBAL/KEEP filename). Initially, the displayed current directory and the default directory are the same. As you browse to another directory, the displayed current directory displays that new directory. Note that you do not have to change the data directory to be able to select a filename form the displayed current directory. Use F3 to change the displayed current directory as required.

f) This is part of the documentation for the spreadsheet. Give TWO reasons why this is not good documentation. *(2 marks)*

Total marks - 20.

SEG

38 A sports club has about 3000 members. Each member pays a yearly fee to use the sports facilities and receive a monthly newsletter. The sports management is thinking of buying an information technology (IT) system to help to increase membership and to speed up the paperwork. The management hopes to be ready in three months' time with the new computerised system fully working.

You are part of the management team.

a) Outline the main steps the management should go through to be ready to install the new working system with the necessary documentation. *(5 marks)*

b) Explain how the team should work together to be ready in three months' time. *(6 marks)*

c) Design a short questionnaire (of no more than five questions) to find members' views of the monthly newsletter. *(5 marks)*

d) Describe ways in which the management team can find out which IT system would be best suited to their needs. *(7 marks)*

e) Explain why some of these ways will be better than others. *(4 marks)*

f) The hardware and software of the new system have been purchased and correctly installed. Describe, in detail, a way in which this new system should handle each of the following.

the members' personal data *(10 marks)*
production of the monthly newsletter *(10 marks)*
actual visits to the sports club by members *(8 marks)*

Give reasons for your answers.

g) After several months of operation, the management decides to enhance the IT system by putting the payroll on it for both full-time and part-time staff.

(i) Discuss the benefits and drawbacks of doing this.

(8 marks)

(ii) Discuss, in detail, how the new hardware and software should operate. *(12 marks)*

Total marks - 30.

MEG

39 An information system controls the number of ships in a harbour.

a) (i) Using these variables, explain how the information system works out how many ships are in the harbour. *(2 marks)*

Variable	Description
SHIPS_IN	The number of ships that go into the harbour.
SHIPS_OUT	The number of ships that leave the harbour.
SHIPS_AT_START	The number of ships at the start of the day.

(ii) The data for the information system can be collected using a manual method or an automatic method. Describe a suitable manual method and a suitable automatic method. *(2 marks)*

b) When the harbour is full, the information system turns on a flashing light at the harbour entrance.

(i) The information system needs to know when the harbour is full. What further information does the computer need to determine whether the harbour is full? *(1 mark)*

(ii) Explain how the information system knows when the harbour is full. *(2 marks)*

c) The harbour inspector tests the information system to make sure it works. Describe TWO tests that should be made. *(2 marks)*

Total marks - 9.

SEG

40

a) In order to access the pupil database, teachers can log onto the network at a remote station from anywhere in the school.

(i) State THREE advantages to the teacher of using such a system compared to manual methods of retrieving the same information. *(3 marks)*

(ii) State TWO steps involved in the logging on at a remote station of the network which has already been switched on.
(4 marks)

b) When a pupil database in initially set up, the required information is collected via the form tutors, primary school record cards and the pupils themselves.

(i) Describe ONE means of capturing data which will help Mrs Collins, the school secretary, collect her information for the database. *(2 marks)*

Mrs Collins' database contains information about each pupil's surname, forename, date of birth, address, tutor group and home telephone number.

(ii) Suggest THREE other fields that could be added to the database. *(3 marks)*

Each year, some of the records will need to be updated or amended.

(iii) Describe what is meant by 'updating' or 'amending' records.
(2 marks)

c) Members of staff often take data from the school database system for integration with their own departmental records.

(i) Describe in detail how this task could be successfully carried out. *(3 marks)*

(ii) Describe FOUR areas a user guide should contain to help all teachers capture and integrate this data. *(4 marks)*

d) A pupil wishes to develop an information retrieval system capable of electronically accessing data from various encyclopaedias, other databases, mailboxes and other sources. The data must then be integrated into a package capable of producing text and graphics.

(i) Describe how such a system might work. *(2 marks)*

(ii) Apart from a computer and printer, identify TWO pieces of hardware and TWO pieces of software which would be required and justify your choice for each. *(4 marks)*

(iii) Fully explain how the data could be captured, entered and processed. *(3 marks)*

(iv) Describe how the system could be tested and refined prior to full implementation taking place. *(2 marks)*

Total marks - 32.

RSA

41 A school wishes to know who owns the cars in the school car park. You are asked to set up a database.

a) Design a questionnaire to collect the data needed. *(4 marks)*

b) You have to set up the fields in each record in the database.

Describe the two most important fields by filling in the table.

(4 marks)

Description of field	Field length	Field type	Example of data

c) The information on the questionnaire is input to the computer by a secretary. The same information is input again by a second secretary. The computer compares the information input by the first secretary and the information input by the second secretary. If both copies of the information are not the same, the computer displays an error message. The secretaries have to find the mistake and correct it.

(i) Complete the sentence using a term from the list.

artificial intelligence
buffering
lexical analysis
validation
verification

Comparing the input by the first secretary and the information input by the second secretary is called
----------------------.
(1 mark)

(ii) Write down ONE advantage to the school in having both secretaries input the information.

d) The database is saved on hard disk. Describe what must be done so that the database will not be lost even if the hard disk is damaged.
(2 marks)

e) Describe ONE way this database would be useful in the school.

f) There are only 12 at the school who have cars. Explain why a computer should not be used to hold the database. *(2 marks)*

Total marks - 16.

SEG

42 Unitas Air is an international airline. Unitas Air holds personal information about its passengers on an international computer network.

a) Describe ONE advantage and ONE disadvantage to a passenger because Unitas Air holds this personal information.
(2 marks)

b) Unitas Air holds information about flight bookings on a large mainframe computer. This mainframe computer is in Spain. Travel agents throughout Europe can book flights by connecting the computers in their shops to this mainframe computer.
Draw a diagram of a Wide Area Network (WAN) that could be used, showing how the computers are connected to the mainframe computer. *(4 marks)*

c) Describe TWO methods Unitas Air could use to prevent unauthorised access to personal information about its passengers. *(2 marks)*

d) Complete these sentences.
The information system used by Unitas Air was designed by a ---------------------------------.
An employee who looks after the mainframe computer while it is running the flight bookings information system is called a ---------------------------------. *(2 marks)*

Total marks - 10.
SEG

43 Mrs Brown is the owner of a small corner shop called 'Triangle Stores'. The business is growing steadily. Present sales include: groceries, newspapers, magazines and video rentals. Mrs Brown needs to develop her newspaper rounds and has decided to ask her customers some questions such as:

What is your name and address?
What newspapers do you buy?
How often do you buy a newspaper?

a) (i) Suggest TWO further questions that Mrs Brown might ask. *(2 marks)*
(ii) Explain how they might be useful when processed by a computer. *(2 marks)*

b) (i) Name the type of software package which would be most suitable to analyse the results of the questionnaire. *(1 mark)*
(ii) Give TWO reasons for your choice. *(2 marks)*

c) How should Mrs Brown organise the structure of the file to give easy entry and analysis of the responses? Give reasons for your answer. *(4 marks)*

d) Identify THREE things Mrs Brown could do to ensure that the data remains secure once she has computerised her customers' survey answers. *(3 marks)*

Fig. 1

e) Identify TWO reasons why it is necessary to ensure the security of customers' personal data. *(2 marks)*

f) A recent break-in and growing losses from shop-lifting have made it necessary for Mrs Brown to consider the need for shop security. Suggest different ways in which electronic systems might be used to help solve the issues of security. *(3 marks)*

g) Most products in the shop have printed codes on them as shown in Fig. 1.
    Describe TWO ways in which these codes might be of use to Mrs Brown in the future. *(6 marks)*

City and Guilds

44

a) The Headteacher of a school, Mr Williams, keeps personal information about his teaching staff on computer. This contains details regarding salaries and responsibilities amongst other things. All staff have a right to see their own personal details held on the computer.

(i) Give TWO reasons why Mr Williams should not allow staff to see the personal details of others. *(2 marks)*

(ii) Give TWO reasons why a school might wish to record personal information about its staff or pupils on a computer compared to manual methods. *(2 marks)*

b) Mr Williams feels that he is able to control how he budgets the school's finances much more easily by using information technology.

(i) Give TWO positive effects which information technology has possibly had on how Mr Williams budgets the school's finances. *(4 marks)*

(ii) Give THREE negative effects which information technology has possibly had on how Mr Williams budgets the school's finances. *(3 marks)*

c) Mr Williams is keen to see information technology being used right across the school in order to benefit all who wish to use it.

(i) Give ONE example of how information could be more readily available to staff with regard to each of the following:
    accuracy of the information
    speed of access to the information *(2 marks)*

(ii) Explain THREE ways in which pupils could benefit from gaining access to information by using the school's network. *(3 marks)*

The Data Protection Act was created for a specific purpose.

(iii) Describe the main purpose of this Act. *(1 mark)*

(iv) Briefly describe ONE recommendation of the Act.
    (1 mark)

d) There is a danger that information stored on the school's computer could be wrongly used more easily than manually recorded data.

    (i) State TWO possible misuses of this information. *(2 marks)*

    (ii) State TWO steps which should be taken to prevent misuse from happening. *(2 marks)*

    (iii) Identify a group of people or an individual who might misuse this information and give ONE reason why they might do so. *(3 marks)*

Total marks - 25.

RSA

45 An office employs many people doing clerical work such as typing and keeping accounts. A large mainframe computer is used to produce the payroll for these staff.

a) Discuss TWO different ways in which the hours worked by these staff could be input into the computer's payroll system, pointing out any benefits and drawbacks of each. *(6 marks)*

b) (i) The system has just been improved to allow the staff to send electronic messages to each other and to process the orders automatically with the suppliers. Discuss the implications of this for the clerical staff. *(4 marks)*

    (ii) The office management is considering allowing staff to have access to the mainframe computer from the terminals on their desks. Discuss the implications of this for the office management. *(6 marks)*

c) Explain the rights that members of staff have concerning their personal data stored for the payroll system. *(4 marks)*

46 A robot is used to weld panels onto vans. The robot has a welding torch attached to it. A computer controls the robot. You give the computer commands and the robot obeys them

a) (i) These are the commands that control the robot. You can change the number of units moved.

Command	Meaning of command
UP 3	Move the welding torch up 3 units
DOWN 2	Move the welding torch down 3 units
LEFT 5	Move the welding torch left 5 units
RIGHT 4	Move the welding torch right 4 units
WELD ON	Start welding
WELD OFF	Stop welding

The robot has to weld from A to B along the dashed line shown. The robot starts at R and should be returned to R. Write the commands to make the robot weld from A to B along the dashed line shown.   *(4 marks)*

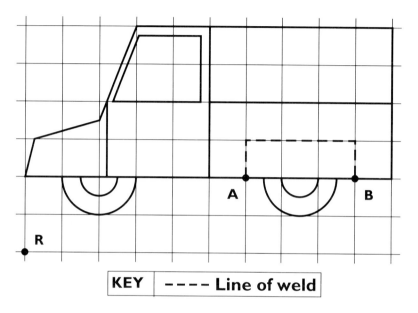

KEY   - - - - **Line of weld**

(ii) Complete the sentence using a term from the list.

batch processing
friction feed
multiprogramming
real time processing
teletext

The computer that controls the robot must run the program using ------------------------------.   *(1 mark)*

b) The welding torch the robot uses can get too hot.
(i) Explain how the computer can know how hot the welding torch is.   *(2 marks)*
(ii) Complete the sentence using a term from the list.

back-up
feedback
hacking
security
over-load

The computer switches the welding torch off when it is too hot. When the welding torch has cooled down, the computer switches it on again. The process must use -----------------------.   *(1 mark)*

c) Welding can be done by a robot or a human welder.
(i) Describe ONE situation where it is better to use a robot welder.   *(1 mark)*

     (ii)   Describe ONE situation where a human welder should do the welding. *(1 mark)*

d)   Using robots can lead to human welders becoming unemployed. Are manufacturing companies sensible to use v｟lders. Give a reasoned argument to support your view. *(4 marks)*

Total marks - 14.

SEG

47 Fill in the blanks in each of the sentences below. Choose the correct words from the following list.

data capture form	data logging	joystick
magnetic strip	MICR	mouse
OCR	OMR	screen (VDU)

a)   The account number on a cheque is read using --------------------.

b)   Data on changes in air temperature is collected automatically using ----------------------- equipment.

c)   Credit cards and bank cards have a ------------------------ which holds account data.

d)   Answers to multiple choice examinations are input to the computer system using ---------------------. *(4 marks)*

NEAB

48 A birdwatcher makes notes in a diary to record findings.

> The jackdaw can be found in England. It is about 30 cms in length, which is smaller than a rook (or crow). It has a grey neck. Its nest is made of sticks lined with grass and wool. The nest can be found on some cliffs and also in trees. The nest I found was on 2 April 1995 and had 4 eggs, which were bluish with dark brown spots.

a)   Describe how you would structure this information as a record in a new database which you are about to create on your computer. *(10 marks)*

b)   Give TWO reasons why it is necessary to structure data in this way. *(2 marks)*

c)   Explain the advantages of CD-ROMs over floppy disks for storing this kind of data. *(4 marks)*

MEG

49 A large firm uses a computer system to handle its payroll operation. The system uses a master file and a transaction file. These are some of the data items stored:

bank account number   employee address
employee number   hours worked this month
pay rate   tax code
total pay to date   total tax to date

a) (i) Name the one item which you would expect to be present in both the master file and the transaction file.   *(1 mark)*
  (ii) Explain why this item would have to be in both files.
                                                        (1 mark)

  (iii) Choose four items which would only be present in the master file.   *(4 marks)*

b) How could the system check that the data entered for number of 'hours worked this month' is always sensible?   *(2 marks)*

c) When the payslips are produced batch processing is used.
  (i) What type of access to the files is required during batch processing?   *(1 mark)*
  (ii) Describe the method of backup which would be used to make sure that if some of the files were damaged they could be restored.   *(4 marks)*

d) The payments to employees are made by transmitting the necessary data to the bank. The bank then transfers money into each employee's bank account.
  (i) The data is encrypted before transmission. Why is this done?   *(1 mark)*
  (ii) What data about each employee would have to be transmitted to allow payment to be made?   *(2 marks)*

Glossary

access time The time taken to find a track and sector on a disk

actuator A device which produces a response to data from sensors

advanced telemetry linked acquisition systems (ATLAS) Software used to collect and log data from sensors

algorithm A plan showing the steps needed to solve a problem or carry out a task

alphanumeric Characters are limited to letters or numbers, usually refers to a database field

analogue A quantity which varies continuously, without fixed gaps between values. An example is temperature

analysis Examining a task or problem to find out what is required to produce a solution

archive file A copy of a file which is kept in case reference has to be made to it, often needed for legal reasons

arithmetic and logic unit (ALU) The part of the CPU where arithmetic takes place and logical comparisons are made

ASCII American Standard Code for Information Interchange, the most commonly used binary code for characters

automated data entry A method of inputting data into a computer using a reading device

automated teller machine (ATM) A cash-point machine which allows certain banking processes to be carried out

back-up copy A copy of data or programs, in computer readable form, kept in case the working copy is damaged

backing store A means of storing large amounts of data outside the computer's memory, e.g. disk, tape

bad sector A part of a disk which is faulty and cannot be used

bar code reader A device used to read data encoded in a bar code by detecting the width of the bars

batch file A file of instructions in the operating system command language, often used to install software or to start up an application

batch processing Processing which only takes place when all inputs (data and programs) have been collected together

bench testing Testing individual parts or special settings in a workshop

binary number A number consisting only of ones and zeros

bit A single binary digit

bit-mapped format A format used for storing graphics files. Data about each point in the image is stored, together with palette data

byte A unit of storage, enough to hold one character

cash-on-delivery item Goods sent without payment and paid for on receipt

central processing unit (CPU) The main part of the computer, consisting of control unit, ALU, and some memory

check digit An extra digit, calculated from the other digits in the data item and added to the end of it. Check digits are used to validate data, e.g in bar codes

clock card A card inserted into a special machine and used to record hours worked

closed loop control system A control system in which there is feedback but no user input

command An instruction to the computer

computer aided design and manufacturing (CAD/CAM) A system in which an article is designed using computer software and then produced using computer-controlled cutting equipment such as a lathe

concurrent assembly mock-up (CAMU) A system allowing simulation of fitting together of parts of a mechanical device to find out how they interact

continuous paper Printer paper supplied as sheets attached to each other but easily separated at perforations

control software Programs used to control external devices

control unit A part of the CPU, controls timing and execution of individual instructions

copyright law Law forbidding unauthorised copying of software and other material

daisy wheel printer An impact printer in which character patterns are placed at the tip of the spokes of a wheel and rotated into position when needed

data Information removed from its context and encoded for computer use

Data Protection Act Act of Parliament controlling use of personal data

data protection principles Rules which a data user must obey

Data Protection Registrar Official responsible for enforcing the Data Protection Act

data subject A living person about whom data, in computer readable form, is held

data table Alternative name for a file in a relational database

data user A person or organisation who uses personal data

data-logging Collecting and storing data at regular, fixed intervals over a period of time

demodulation Extracting the original digital signal from the modulated transmitted signal

demultiplexing Separating individual signals from signals combined for transmission

device driver Software needed to make a device such as a printer work correctly

digital signal A signal representing a series of binary ones and zeros

direct access Ability to read or write to any known location in storage without access to preceding locations first

direct access file A file in which locations of records are known so that they can be read or written in any order

disaster recovery plan A scheme which will allow provision of hardware and recovery of data in the event of loss of computer resources

disk Storage medium, magnetic or optical

disk directory A list of all the files stored on the disk, usually divided into subdirectories

disk drive Device which writes data to, and reads data from, a disk

distribution disks The disks on which a software package is supplied

documentation Written information about a computer system. It is usually divided into user documentation and maintenance documentation

dot matrix printer impact printer which builds up characters or graphics from dots produced by firing pins at the paper and ribbon

electronic funds transfer (EFT) Used to transfer money between accounts immediately

electronic mail system Using computers to transfer messages between users. Messages are held in a central store until read

electronic point of sale (EPOS) System used in shops to read bar codes and look up prices, often linked to stock control systems

encryption Altering data stored on disk or transmitted from one computer to another so that it makes no sense if it is stolen

end-of-field marker A special character used to mark the end of a variable length field in a data file

error report A listing of all errors which have occurred during processing

European article number (EAN) A system of numbering products, internationally agreed, used in producing bar codes for retail goods

exemption (from Data Protection Act) Grounds on which data may be excluded from the provisions of the Data Protection Act

feasibility report A written statement in which the likely costs and benefits of a proposed system are evaluated

Federation Against Software Theft An organisation which works to find those who use illegal copies of software

field A single data item in a record

file A collection of related records

file compression Reducing the size of a file by removing redundant characters

file format The way data is stored on a disk

formatting Writing track and sector data onto a disk before it can be used

gateway A node on a network which allows communication between terminals on different networks

gigabyte A thousand million bytes, unit used to measure memory and backing store

hacker A person who makes illegal access to a computer system

hacking The process of gaining illegal access to a computer system

human computer interface The way in which humans and computers communicate

hypertext link text which provides links to other pages in an information store

immediate access store (IAS) the memory of a computer system, also called primary store

impact printer A printer which produces output by hitting pins or a character pattern against paper and a ribbon

Information Superhighway A system which will allow rapid access to on-line data using fast cable connections and high speed telecommunications links

ink-jet printer A printer which produces its output by spraying minute drops of ink and directing them onto the paper

input device A device which allows data to be transferred to the computer

Internet A world-wide network of networks

IP address An individual address on the Internet

keyboard An input device used to type characters, the codes for which are transmitted to the computer

kilobyte 1024 bytes

Kimball tag A small punched card containing a limited amount of encoded data, still used in some clothes shops

laser printer A page printer in which the image is formed using a laser and electrostatic attraction of toner

line printer An impact printer which produces a whole line of text in one operation

local area network A network in which the component parts are linked by cables

log file A file containing details of all changes made to stored data

magnetic ink character recognition (MICR) System used in banking to input data from cheques

magneto-optical disk A disk which allows read and write access by combining magnetic and optical methods of storage

mail-merging Inserting fields from a database file into a standard letter to produce personalised copies

master file A file containing data not usually subject to frequent change. It is the principal source of information for a computing job

medium Anything on which data is stored or printed

megabyte One million bytes, a unit of storage for memory and backing store

menu-based system A system in which the user is offered a series of menus from which to choose the required tasks

microfiche An output medium consisting of sheets of microfilm which can be read in a special reader

modem A modulator/demodulator which converts digital data for transmission along telephone connections and extracts the digital data from received signals

modulation The process of converting a digital signal for transmission over a telephone line

monitor Also called VDU, the screen on which output is displayed

monitor To read input from a sensor at regular intervals

monitoring software A program which reads sensor input and usually activates controlling devices. The data read is often stored for analysis later

mouse An input device used to provide positional data and to select choices

multi-programming system A system which appears to run more than one program at once

multi-user system A system in which many users all share the CPU of one computer. It works by giving each user a short time slice

multiplexor A device which combines many signals for transmission

network A collection of linked computers, able to share resources

network topology The way in which the terminals in a LAN are connected

newsgroups Groups of news articles or messages about a particular topic on the Internet

node A network terminal

non-impact printer A printer which produces its image without hammering anything against the paper

non-volatile memory Memory which does not lose its contents when the computer is turned off (ROM)

numeric Data consisting entirely of numbers

object An item created in software which has definite properties associated with it. Often consists of many parts but is treated as a single item

operating system A program or group of programs which controls the entire operation of the computer

optical character recognition (OCR) A method of data input in which reflected light is used to detect character patterns

optical disk A disk which is read using a laser beam

optical mark recognition (OMR) Input of data by detecting marks on a form. Light reflection is used to detect the marks and they are interpreted as data by software

output device Any device which receives and displays data from a computer

palette The particular collection of colours in use at any time

parity bit A bit within a data byte which is set to make the total number of ones either odd (for odd parity) or even (for even parity). Used to detect changes in data as it moves from one medium to another

parity check The process of checking that the parity bits in received data are correct

parity track The area on paper tape or magnetic tape which is used to hold the parity bits

partial exemption (from Data Protection Act) A situation in which some provisions of the Data Protection Act do not apply

password A code or word which must be entered before access to data is allowed

password hierarchy A system in which different passwords give different levels of access to data

peripherals Devices (input, output or storage) which are attached to a computer

personal data Data about a living person, identifiable from the data held

personal identification number (PIN) A number giving access to cashpoint or other banking facilities, used to prevent fraud

pixel A single point in an image on screen

plotter An output device which draws charts or diagrams using pens

point of presence A connection point, usually a local phone number, to an Internet service supplier

presence check A validation check which ensures that a field contains data

primary key field A field in a database file which contains a unique value for each record. Allows an individual record to be identified

primary storage The memory of a computer system

print queue A list of files waiting to be printed. As each job is completed the next begins

protocol A defined method of making a connection between two computers

random access memory (RAM) Volatile memory, the contents of which can be changed by the user

range check A validation check designed to ensure a value lies within a specified range

rational database management system Software which manages linked data tables and processes queries

read only memory (ROM) Non volatile memory, contents are not lost when the computer is switched off. Used to store system software

read-only access Restricts user access to data files so that records can be read but not altered

real time processing Processing in which incoming data is handled rapidly enough for outputs to affect further inputs to the system

record A collection of data about a person or thing, one element in a file

redundancy Having more processing power and other resources than are necessary for normal processing. Common in real-time systems

report Printed output from a database

requirement specification A list of tasks a system must carry out if it is to be regarded as successful. May also include various constraints on the system

resolution The number of dots per inch displayed on a screen or printed by a printer

scanner Input device which is used to convert an image to digital data

search path The directory path used in looking for a specified file

sector Part of a track on a disk surface. Data is transferred one sector at a time

sensor Electronic device which responds to variations in environmental conditions by generating a varying signal

sequential Data is processed in the order in which it was stored but it is stored in a logical order, e.g. alphabetically

serial access Data is processed in the order in which it was stored. No ordering is present

service provider An organisation which provides access to the Internet or other communications facilities

simulation Using a computer to model a situation or process, usually with realistic output

smart card A plastic card which can store data and on which the data can be altered during use

software piracy Using or selling software in breach of licence agreements

storage device A device such as a disk or tape drive which stores data

subdirectory A branch of the main directory of a disk

system flowchart A diagram which shows flow of data through a system

system test Testing designed to find out if the whole of the system works as it should

system utility program A program, usually supplied with the operating system, which carries out a routine system task

tape Plastic strip coated with magnetisable material, used to store data

tape drive Device which writes data to and reads data from a tape

tape streamer A device used in backup. Data is copied to tape held in a small cartridge

telemetry Transmission of signals from remote sensors to a computer

terminal A computer or workstation attached to a network

test data Data designed to test a system, usually includes typical, extreme and erroneous values

thermal printer A printer which produces an image by heating the paper

token An electronic signal used to establish connections in some local area networks

toner A powder used to produce the printed image on a laser printer

track A circular area on a disk or a linear area on a tape in which data is stored

transaction file A sequential file used to update a master file during batch processing

transaction log file A sequential file containing details of all changes made to a direct access file

transposition error An error in which two digits of a number are swapped over

tree A data structure in which there is a series of divisions or choices, e.g. directory tree

type check Check to make sure that data entered is of the appropriate type, e.g. numeric

validation check Ensures that data entered is sensible and reasonable

verification check Ensures that data entered has been transcribed correctly

virus Code which replicates itself and is transmitted from one machine to another attached to other files. Usually designed to damage data

visual display unit (VDU) Screen used to display computer output

volatile memory Contents are lost when the computer is switched off

web browser Software used to access Internet pages by means of hypertext links

wide area network Network in which computers are linked using communications lines such as phone lines instead of cables

wire-frame model Graphic representation of an object using lines instead of a shaded, solid-looking image

Index

Acknowledgements

The authors would like to thank the following individuals and organisations for their help in writing this book:

McLaren International Motor Racing Ltd, NatWest Bank plc, a Medical Centre in north-east England, the Urban Traffic Control Department of Cleveland County Council, and Mr M. Woods.

The authors and publishers would like to thank the following companies, individuals and institutions who gave permission to reproduce photographs in this book:

Brian Capon/British Bankers Association (11 top, 12, 77); Mondex UK (78, 79 both); Paul Seheult/Eye Ubiquitous (8 left, 10); Sporting Pictures UK Ltd (86, 89, 91); TAG/McLaren Marketing Services (88 both); Trip/H. Rogers (1, 2, 3 both, 5 both, 6, 8 right, 10, 11 bottom, 13, 17 all, 19 both, 21, 22 all, 23 both, 24 both, 25 both, 26, 27 both, 28 both, 34, 41, 50, 56, 61, 62 both, 63 both, 66, 81, 82). With grateful thanks to Asda Stores, Bytes Computers and Stratacom Computers for their assistance.

We would also like to thank the following bodies who gave permission to reproduce copyright question material:

Midland Examining Group, Southern Examining Group, Northen Examinations Assessment Board, RSA Examinations Board, and the City and Guilds of London Institute.

The pages were designed by Graphic Designer, Fiona Webb and the illustrations were produced by GDN Associates. The cover and title pages for *This is IT!* and this book were designed by Liz Rowe with artwork by David Atkinson. Thanks also to Penni Bickle, freelance picture researcher, and David Page for their work on this book and *This is IT!*.

Other resources

▇ *This is IT!*

Hodder and Stoughton, 1995. 160 pp. ISBN 0340 61104 9.

Also written by Anne Ramkaran and Ian Ithurralde, *This is IT!* fulfils the requirements for the new National Curriculum Orders at Key Stages 3 and 4. It is also a useful introduction to GNVQ core skills in IT at Intermediate Level.

Used together, *This is IT!* and *This is IS!* provide full coverage of most GCSE syllabuses in Information Technology and Information Systems.

This is IT! is designed to help students find effective IT solutions by understanding the design process and then applying appropriate skills to the problem. Free-standing chapters cover the main packages most likely to be used by students, with tasks to guide their learning. Further chapters cover a range of applications of IT and explore the impact of IT on society.

As in *This is IS!*, each chapter contains short questions for students to check their understanding of the topics covered. Longer exam questions are also included for practice at the end of most chapters.

This is IT! is divided into four sections covering the following topics:

Communicating and Handling Information
Information and data
Handling information
Databases, word processing, graphics, DTP and sound

Using IT to investigate
Spreadsheets, and using spreadsheets for modelling
Simulation software
Measurement and control

Selecting and Developing Information Systems
Evaluating software
Producing and documenting systems

IT in Society
IT in a medical centre, an urban traffic control system and a supermarket
IT in society

This IT! CD-ROM

Hodder and Stoughton, 1995. ISBN 0340 64344 7.

The CD-ROM has been developed jointly by the authors of *This is IT!* and *This is IS!* and the Cleveland Educational Computing Centre. It ties in with both students' books and is intended to be used as a resource by IT co-ordinators, but is also useful for teachers in other curriculum areas.

The disk contains a variety of interactive databases, images, spreadsheets, exam questions and activity worksheets for students, which can be customised to fit teachers' requirements. It also contains advice on preparing for OFSTED inspections, IT policy and planning and differentiation.

It will run on both PC and Archimedes systems.

This is IT! and *This is IS!* can both be ordered on inspection. A free information pack is available to evaluate the CD-ROM (ISBN 0340 61100 6). Please contact:

Bookpoint Ltd
Hodder and Stoughton Educational
Direct Services
FREEPOST OF 1488
Abingdon
Oxon OX14 4YY

Credit card hotline: 01235 400405.